John F. Kennedy

by **Richard Tregaskis**

and PT-109

Random House, New York

To a dedicated and gifted leader, J.F.K.

Author's acknowledgment I have consulted with many of the people named in this narrative in order to obtain and check my facts; namely, Al Cluster, Les Gamble, Commander Tom Kendall, Bob Wark, Admiral A. P. Calvert, Homer Facto, Commander Henry J. Brantingham. I also want to express maximum gratitude for help in my research to the following: Pierre Salinger, Admiral Samuel Eliot Morison, Charlie Bloch and Bob Specht; Commander Russ Bufkins and the staff at Navy Public Information Office Headquarters, Washington, D.C.; Mrs. Mildred D. Mayeux and Dean C. Allard, Jr., at the Navy Records Center; Admiral Ernest T. Eller, Navy Historian; Lieutenant Colonel Bud Kilgore, Colonel Walter Griscti at CINCPAC. *R.T.*

Picture credits Endpaper and title page: official U. S. Navy photographs.

Library of Congress Catalog Card Number: 62–9009

Manufactured in the United States of America

Contents

John F. Kennedy

Young John (second from right in the front row) poses with the football team at Choate School.
[United Press]

John Kennedy at the age of 21 boards a plane in London with his father, Joseph P. Kennedy (right).
[United Press]

Lt. Kennedy is congratulated by Capt. F. L. Conklin (left) after receiving the Navy and Marine Corps Medal for gallantry in action.

[United Press]

President Kennedy at the White House chats with Arthur R. Evans, the Australian coastwatcher responsible for Kennedy's rescue from Cross Island. They are holding the note written by Evans and later framed as a memento by Kennedy.

[Wide World]

PT Maneuvers and Training

From the cockpit of his lead boat, Lt. Comdr. Alan Montgomery (left) works out tactics and transmits them to the rest of his PT training squadron.   [Wide World]

Traveling at high speed a squadron of mosquito boats practices wartime maneuvers in the Panama Canal Zone. [Wide World]

During training a group of officers aboard a PT boat inspect the craft's supply of depth bombs.

[Wide World]

A great geyser of water rises above the explosion of a depth charge dropped a few seconds earlier by a speedy motor torpedo boat.

[Wide World]

A PT boat throws out a smoke screen before firing on an enemy base.

[U.S. Navy]

U. S. Mosquito Boats Invade
the Solomon Islands

An aerial view of Tulagi island, a PT base in the Solomons. [U.S. Navy]

Enlisted men of the PT flotilla which operated during World War II in the Guadalcanal area walk to their camp on Florida Island.

[Wide World]

PT crewmen make repairs while their boat is tied alongside the mother ship. [Wide World]

A mosquito boat, screened by tropical foliage and camouflaged by paint and netting, hides out near the flotilla base. [Wide World]

A Japanese destroyer with its characteristic upside-down Y-shaped funnels.
[Wide World]

Kohei Hanami, commander of the Japanese destroyer *Amagiri* at the time it crashed into PT-109.
[Wide World]

A PT gunner on night patrol draws a bead with his twin .50-caliber machine guns.

John F. Kennedy and PT-109

I.

A Lieutenant Joins the PTs

At 1:43 on the morning of Sunday, August 9, 1942, the cannonading began. Men of the First Marine Raider Battalion saw the flashes against the rainy night sky to the southwest. But they did not stir from their sleeping places, for it was a rule among the marines that anything moving at night would be shot at.

After two days of hard fighting, the Raiders had virtually secured the tiny island of Tulagi, across the bay from Guadalcanal in the South Pacific. Colonel Merritt A. "Red Mike" Edson's First Marine Raider Battalion had encountered suicidally determined resistance from the tough defending Japanese forces dug into the caves and ravines of jungly Tulagi. And through the night there had been occasional crackling outbursts of small-arms fire as marines fired at isolated enemy snipers, real or imagined. But for the most part, the island of Tulagi—once the seat of British colonial government in the Solomon Islands—had been quiet until the cannonading broke out.

The men looked up from the foxholes they had dug, or peered out the windows of the few remaining shacks which had not been smashed by the fighting. Tired eyes, gleaming white in faces begrimed by two days of sweating, fighting and suffering in the jungle, watched the greenish-white flashes. Ears keyed to the slightest of sounds listened to the steady *brroom-brroom* of the distant cannons.

As the Raiders listened and watched, they realized that a major sea battle was being waged somewhere between Tulagi and Guadalcanal. They sensed that their future was being settled among the green flashes and metallic thunderings of the naval guns. As the crashing of the guns increased in tempo, it also grew louder, and seemed to be moving toward Tulagi. Then, at about 2:30 A.M., the flickering lights began to fade in the sky, and the thunder of guns grew fainter. No one on Tulagi knew whether the lull in the heavy firing meant that the engagement was over or would renew itself with mounting fury a second later.

Not until years later, when the war was over, were the facts of this First Battle of Savo Island known. Japanese Admiral Mikawa, in his flagship *Chokai,* had led a marauding force of Japanese cruisers and destroyers into "The Slot" between Guadalcanal and Savo Island. Here he had pounced upon the unaware force of American cruisers and destroyers supposedly guarding the transport ships which had just landed the Marine forces invading the islands of Guadalcanal, Tulagi, Gavutu and Tanambogo.

Mikawa's forces had quickly made expert torpedo and gunnery attacks, and left four Allied heavy cruisers burning—the United States ships *Quincy, Astoria* and *Vincennes,* and the pride of the Australian Pacific navy, the *Canberra.* During the night, all four were to sink, with a loss of more than 1,000 lives. The engagement was the first of the many violent sea battles to rage in the waters around the Solomon Islands.

Back in the United States very little information was reaching the public beyond the brief Navy communiqués reporting that marines had landed in the Solomon Islands at Guadalcanal, Tulagi and Gavutu. But at the very moment when the marines on Tulagi were wondering about the meaning of the naval action out there in the dark, a small group of men at the Brooklyn Navy Yard in New York was making its own contribution to eventual victory for America.

At the Navy yard, 10,000 miles away from the Solomons, it was 11:30 A.M., bright midday. And the crew of PT Boat 109 (PT meaning Patrol Torpedo) had just taken a hard-earned lunch break from their work of fitting out PT-109 at the Brooklyn yard. PT-109 was one of the latest models of a so-called "miracle weapon" —an 80-foot plywood-and-mahogany speedboat armed with torpedoes and machine guns. General Douglas MacArthur had said this weapon might have made a considerable difference in the defense of the Philippines if it had been available in much larger quantities. Now, four months after the fall of the Philippines to the Japanese war machine, mass production of the PT boats had just begun.

The 109 boat was the sixth of a new class of PTs designed to be mass-produced at the Elco Boat Works at Bayonne, New Jersey. As the crewmen of the 109 boat stopped for lunch, nine more boats in the same series were coming off the Elco production lines, and a hundred more would be built in the next year.

Like Kaiser's Liberty ships, which were built in large sections like automobile parts and assembled on a giant factory line, the Elco 80-footers came together in two major pieces, hull and deckhouse. After the decks were in, a giant hoist lifted the 30-ton hull and swung it into the water. From there it was guided to the giant, hangar-like fitting-out building where the hull would be made into a fighting boat with the addition of two dual .50-caliber gun mounts on the right forward and left rear sections of the deckhouse. Four torpedo tubes, two even with the bridge structure amidship, and two on the afterdeck, were also installed on the boat. Like fat steel crayons, these were oriented fore and aft, so that they were aimed generally in the same direction as the boat. When an attack was to be made, they would be trained out a few degrees. In this way the torpedoes, when fired, would clear the side of the boat. Then, once in the water, they would be trained by gyroscope mechanism so that their course would follow the direction the boat had been pursuing. Besides the .50-caliber dual mounts and the torpedo tubes, some of the boats were equipped with two depth-charge mountings on the bow.

With the mountings of the armor-plated deckhouse, the rakish windshield with its base of armor-plate, the guns, the four torpedo tubes, and the depth-charge cradles, the little plywood "destroyers" began to look more formidable.

In July of 1942, PT-109 was ready to leave the Elco Boat Works. At the Bayonne fitting-out basin, a crew went aboard the spic-and-span new motor torpedo boat and started the short trek down Newark Bay toward New York Harbor and Brooklyn.

At the Brooklyn Navy Yard the fitting out of the PT boat was completed and she was taken on a series of shake-down cruises. PT-109 had been routinely assigned to Ensign Bryant L. Larson as part of a squadron of six new boats under the command of Lieutenant Commander Clifton B. Maddox. The squadron was as yet unassigned but rumor had it that they would be sent to action in the South Pacific.

At this time the Navy skipper who was later to win fame for his command of PT-109 had not the slightest inkling that she would ever be his boat. A tall, slim, intense young man with gray eyes and a pug nose, he was attending the Naval Reserve Officers' Training School at Northwestern University, Chicago. John Fitzgerald Kennedy was one of tens of thousands of young American men wearing the single gold bar of ensign.

This young freckle-faced, mop-haired ensign

differed from the average, however, in that he bore a famous name. His father, Joseph P. Kennedy, a Boston multimillionaire, had until recently been American Ambassador to the Court of St. James, at that time considered America's top diplomatic post.

John Kennedy, the second oldest son of former Ambassador Kennedy, had succeeded in joining the naval service in October of 1941. He had tried unsuccessfully to volunteer for duty in the Army. But the Army had rejected him on account of a back injury incurred while he was playing junior varsity football at Harvard University. After his rejection by the Army, he had taken a course of corrective exercises and had at last managed to be accepted as an officer in the U. S. Navy.

His first assignments had been dull ones. The young officer had felt restive and frustrated (especially since his older brother Joe had gone to a fighting front in Europe). John had quickly volunteered his services for a more exciting and dangerous assignment, somewhat nearer the front. But the wheels of bureaucracy, even during wartime, turn very slowly, and weeks went by with no change of assignment.

Finally, at the same time the first communiqués of action in the Solomons were being released, new orders were put in the works for Ensign John F. Kennedy. He was being assigned to the PT training school at Melville, Rhode Island, the Little Annapolis of the torpedo boat squadrons. Some students already called it "Mudville," a newly constructed line of Quonset huts ranged along the shore of Narragansett Bay. But at the time it was the best and only school for officers and crewmen being trained to man the fleet of thunder boats which the United States Navy was to send out into the Solomons area to battle with Japanese destroyers and cruisers.

John Fitzgerald Kennedy had been in many ways well prepared through his twenty-five years of life for the job he was to undertake as a PT skipper and naval officer. Born in Brookline, Massachusetts, on May 29, 1917, he was the second son of a man who had proved to be a financial genius. Consequently young John

grew up in wealthy surroundings, and for rec- ·
reation he was used to sailing small boats at
various yachting centers. He had also acquired
a fine education at Harvard University and the
London School of Economics. It was almost an
automatic requirement for officership in the
armed services that a young man must have at
least two years of college training. And Navy
Procurement always looked for yachting and
motorboating experience in the men they sent
to the PT school at Melville.

As John's father rose in wealth and position,
the family grew rapidly. Besides John and his
brother Joseph, Jr., who was two years older,
there were seven other children. To keep up
with the expanding family, the Kennedy house-
hold moved periodically to larger, more sump-
tuous quarters: to Naples Road in Brookline,
then to Riverdale, New York. After Riverdale,
the family moved to another, still more splendid house in another New York suburb, Bronxville. In the Bronxville estate the lawns were
large enough for the children to play baseball
and football.

In the pleasant environment of large family estates and good schools, John began to build a strong physique, which was to stand him in good stead during his naval service. At preparatory school he tried out for the squad in football and baseball, but his best sport was swimming. When he was thirteen, he could swim fifty yards in thirty seconds which was then, as now, good speed for a boy of that age.

During the summers, John (better known as Jack) had his fill of sailing, swimming and other water sports at the large family summer homes in Palm Beach, Florida, and Hyannis Port on Cape Cod, Massachusetts. The children arranged games of tennis (on the family court), softball, and touch football, but racing sailboats seemed to be the predominant passion of the two oldest boys. At the age of twelve, Jack had his first sailboat, which he named *Victura,* proving that his sailing might have been good and competitive, but that his Latin was lacking something. His intention was to give the boat the Latin name for victory, *Victoria,* but—well,

Latin was his worst subject. In general, in the tough preparatory schools of Canterbury and Choate, his grades were average, sometimes even less than that. At Choate, he graduated 64th in a class of 112.

In his college years, John began to come into his own. He played as a member of the freshman football team (incidentally injuring his back in the process), swam backstroke on the swimming squad; and not only graduated *cum laude* in history, government and economics, but wrote a thesis which won a rating of *magna cum laude*. With some changes and additions, it was published by Wilfred Funk, Inc., under the title *Why England Slept*. On the eve of America's entry into World War II, it became a best seller.

After his graduation in June of 1940, indecision temporarily plagued Jack Kennedy. At first, he planned to study at the Yale Law School. Then he went to California to study at the Business School in Stanford University for six months, and gave that up too. He next set out on a rambling trip through South America (at

the same time the Nazis were successfully attacking and annexing the Balkans and then invading Russia).

By December 7, 1941, the date of the Japanese surprise attack on Pearl Harbor, both John
and his older brother were in the armed services.
Joseph, Jr., had managed to join the Navy as
an officer, and was sent to Britain, where he became involved in a top-secret air operation for
the Navy. Jack, after being turned down by the
Army, took exercises to improve the muscular
tone of his back, which had bothered him so per-
sistently. After being admitted to the Navy and
commissioned as an officer, he was sent to two
dull office jobs: working on plans to defend
defense factories in the event they should be
subjected to aerial attack; and then, after that,
editing a news digest for the Navy staff in Washington. He was next sent to the Naval Reserve
Officers' Training School at Northwestern University, where he was still located in September
when he finally received his orders to report to
the Motor Torpedo Boat Squadron Training
Center in Rhode Island.

2.

The PTs Have Arrived

Meanwhile, something very important to the naval career of John F. Kennedy, and to the future of the desperate battle then raging in the Solomons, had been happening in the Panama Canal Zone. Lieutenant Commander Alan R. Montgomery, one of the few naval officers with PT boat experience and training, had been authorized to form a new torpedo boat squadron. For boats and men he was to draw from the only available stock in the U. S. Navy—eleven old Elco 77-footers and 190 officers and men then assembled at Coco Solo in the Canal Zone.

The boats had been built by painstaking hand methods at the Elco plant during the previous year. They were roughly of the same vintage as the torpedo boats sent out to help General MacArthur in the defense of the Philippines during the early months of 1941. The six boats sent to the Philippines had been called Squadron Three. Under Lieutenant Commander John D. Bulkeley they had reportedly sunk two 5,000-ton Japanese ships—an armed transport and an aircraft tender—as well as several landing barges. They also had hit and damaged a Japanese cruiser, and disabled three enemy aircraft with deck guns. These brave actions had encouraged the American people to fight on in the hour of defeat.

But all of the boats of Squadron Three, and more than two-thirds of the officers and men, had been lost in the Philippine defeat. So the illustrious name of PT Squadron Three was bestowed on the new group of boats and men organized in the Canal Zone.

During the summer of 1942, the boats of Montgomery's 'Ron Three had been practicing, maneuvering, working out kinks and developing team play in the waters around the Canal

Zone. Their tactical practice was based mainly on the experience of Commander Bulkeley's original Squadron Three in the Philippines. The combat reports had been sifted, noted, discussed and digested at Navy headquarters in Washington. The "Book" of school solutions issued to Commander Montgomery, and to the new PT school at Melville, was based on successful attacks made on Japanese transports and auxiliary vessels around Subic Bay.

Honored at being given the designation of a squadron which had acquitted itself so gloriously in the Philippines campaign, the men of 'Ron Three were eager for action on any front. However, they surmised they were most apt to be sent to the South Pacific.

Admiral Ernest J. King, chief of naval operations in Washington, had determined to send every available ounce of naval strength to the Solomon Islands battlefield. He wanted to bolster the position of the marines who had seized ground in the first American land offensive of World War II. In addition to sending all available warships to the Pacific, he ordered a step-up

in PT boat construction and the organization
of PT squadrons. From General MacArthur's
experience in the Philippines, Admiral King
had learned that PT boats could be valuable
for naval operations, both offensive and defen-
sive, in the area of an amphibious landing.

Toward the end of August, Lieutenant Commander Montgomery had his orders to move.
He was not immediately told of his destination,
for it was still a military secret. Specifically he
knew only that the squadron was being sent
into the South Pacific. But by now Montgomery had guessed that his squadron was probably
going to be the first into action in the critical
Solomons campaign.

The last week in August, the squadron began loading four of their eight boats aboard two
Navy oilers, the *Tappahannock* and the *Lackawanna*. Each oiler, or tanker, carried two PTs.
The boats were fastened securely to the forward
and after decks of the tankers, and the squadron
gear that went with them was stowed amidships.
The other four PT boats were loaded aboard a
Liberty ship. The crews—at that time consisting

of two officers and eight men to a boat—made preparations to live aboard the boats during the long voyage. Wires were rigged to the electrical supply of the mother ship, so that they could have power and lights (under blackout conditions) during the trip.

The men were full of fight. They hadn't been able to fire torpedoes (even with dummy warheads) in the congested Panama waters, so they were naturally eager to try them out in actual combat. They were all veterans of long Navy service—selected volunteers with, on the average, eight or ten years in the fleet. Each of them had received from three to five months of training with the PTs. Every crewman could do many jobs aboard his small, fast splinter boat. The cooks were also gunners, and the quartermasters who steered the boats could also, in a pinch, do the work of the torpedomen—and vice versa. The motor machinists (MACS) could take apart and assemble their big Packard engines while half asleep; the gunners could do the same with their dual .50-caliber turret heavy machine guns, and fire them expertly at targets.

The officers at the wheels had learned how to snake among shoals at high speed and could handle their 77-foot speedboats like gocarts. The torpedomen kept their gyros and arming impellers clean and oiled. Even if they couldn't fire their tubes, they could vault to battle stations in the dark and bring mallets to the ready within inches of the firing pins—just as if they were on a fighting run.

Commander Montgomery had built an elite squadron from the reservoir of boats and talent available in the Panama Canal Zone.

On September 18, 1942, Montgomery and his first four boats reached Noumea, New Caledonia, a sunny French colonial seaport 7,000 miles from California and 1,000 miles southeast of Guadalcanal. It had taken them twenty-two days to make the tedious, rough, hot voyage across the ocean to the South Pacific battle area (SOPAC). The second section of four boats was following on the Liberty ship. They didn't reach Noumea until October 25, more than a month after the first four boats arrived.

Noumea was a bustling United States Navy seaport, the largest in the Pacific war area with the exception of Pearl Harbor. An immense, sprawling colony of Quonset huts marked the fact that this was the headquarters of the commander of the South Pacific (COMSOPAC).

The *Tappahannock* came to anchor, and Commander Montgomery went ashore to get his final orders at COMSOPAC and to wage a minor campaign to get the facilities he needed for his boats. He knew he would have to convince the local officials that the PTs were more like aircraft than steel-hulled destroyers. They would need rather intricate maintenance facilities. The boats couldn't be left up some tropical creek in the Guadalcanal vicinity with no base facilities for engine overhaul, for they were equipped with high-tempered aero-type engines. Without some way to repair bent propellers and to clean fouled bottoms, the much-vaunted speed of the PTs could not be preserved.

He got some assurance that facilities would be provided for supply of high-test aviation gasoline and support from Naval Operating Base, Guadalcanal. But beyond that—everything was uncertain in Guadalcanal. At that time nobody could be sure that the Japanese might not dislodge the United States forces from their tiny foothold, the seven-by-two-mile beachhead on the big eighty-mile-long island.

One of the boat commanders, Lieutenant Robert Wark, was flown from Noumea to Guadalcanal to help prepare the PT base at the site of the old British government pier. Montgomery himself went out to the *Tappahannock* and *Lackawanna* to superintend the delicate job of unloading the first four squadron boats by harbor crane from the deck. Noumea was the last base with cranes big enough to tackle the job of hoisting the 65-ton boats into the water. The PT men pitched into the ticklish job and got their boats launched, but not without casualties. There were plenty of bruised bodies and sore skulls by the time the job was done.

The boats were painted a dull forest green, so they would blend with the jungle colors of their future anchorage. Then a cargo ship and

THE PACIFIC ISLAND GROUPS

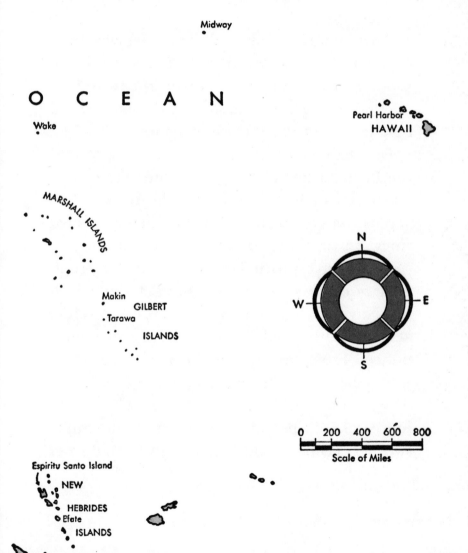

Midway

O C E A N

Wake

Pearl Harbor
HAWAII

MARSHALL ISLANDS

Makin
GILBERT
Tarawa
ISLANDS

N

W ━●━ E

S

0   200   400   600   800
Scale of Miles

Espiritu Santo Island
NEW
HEBRIDES
Efate
ISLANDS

NEW CALEDONIA
Nouméa

an old converted yacht, the *Jamestown,* lined up to tow them north to Espiritu Santo, a primitive base in the New Hebrides. The boats had to be towed, for their gasoline tanks weren't big enough for so long a trip.

Towing was a cruel trial. The steel-wire lines kept parting, and volunteers looped in safety ropes had to scramble over the boat bow to pull up the towing pendant so that the boat could be attached to the tow cable again.

On October 10, the boats were brought into the little harbor of Espiritu Santo. From here on to Guadalcanal, they would be in dangerous waters swarming with enemy submarines, cruisers, destroyers and transports.

Ashore at Espiritu Santo, Commander Montgomery checked in at the Quonset hut which was Navy headquarters. He got orders to refuel at once and be ready to shove off at a moment's notice. From this point forward, the boats would be towed by two racy little former destroyers of World War I vintage. These slim four-stacker ships had been converted into minesweepers (DMSs), and they had just come from

Guadalcanal. Their crew members had the white, haunted eyes, the tight-drawn faces that come from combat.

The two antiquated minesweepers and the PTs had a difficult time after they set out for Guadalcanal on the night of October 11. Again, the wire towropes kept breaking. And in the dark, in heavy seas, this meant that the PT boats had to start their engines and set up a bearing to catch the towship, which couldn't think of stopping in such enemy-infested waters. Then athletic crewmen had to work their way over the seven-foot bow in pitch-blackness.

However, this was not yet war action—only the kind of maneuver the crews had been practicing in the Canal Zone. Now came the real moment, the moment when the blacked-out towships cast the PTs loose in the wide, dark ocean below Indispensable Strait, to the south of Guadalcanal and Tulagi. The boats started their engines and took a bearing for Tulagi and Florida islands, to the north of Guadalcanal. Montgomery's calculation was that the craft would have gas enough to make the rest of the trip under their own power. They would have to travel slow enough to conserve fuel, but fast enough to get to their new base under cover of night.

It was dawn on the morning of October 12 when the four boats turned into the sweep of bay between the dark long coast of Florida Island and the rough green mounds of Tulagi, Gavutu and Tanambogo. Fortunately all of these islands, including Florida, had been cleared of the enemy by this time. The PT crews tied up their boats under the protective foliage of Tulagi and caught up with a few hours of sleep. Then they plunged into the work of setting up such meager facilities as they had for a base. On the shore of Florida Island, the PT men and their assigned base personnel began to erect living quarters at a native village made up largely of primitive thatched huts. The squadron-base people, as well as some of the officers and men, would live in tents and old native huts, while others would be sleeping aboard the boats.

The other part of the PT base consisted of a repair facility at Sesapi on the small island of Tulagi, half a mile away. Here there was a pier, inadequate for the whole PT squadron but large enough for one boat at a time to be secured. On Tulagi, Commander Montgomery reported in to Brigadier General William H. Rupertus, second in command of the Marine force in the Solomons. Then he hopped a ride on a landing boat which took him across Tulagi Bay to the headquarters of Major General Alexander A. Vandegrift on Guadalcanal.

As Montgomery moved around General Vandegrift's muddy headquarters, the report began to circulate that he was commanding officer of a group of PTs which had come in to help defend Guadalcanal from the nightly arrivals of the Tokyo Express. "Tokyo Express" was the marines' nickname for the Japanese warships which came down The Slot between Guadalcanal and Savo islands to land troops, artillery and supplies at Cape Esperance and other Japanese-held points on Guadalcanal. The popular theory was that Montgomery's new, powerful splinter fleet, although composed of only four vessels, would bring magical relief from the Japanese naval supply trains that had been slipping in at night and firing high explosives at the Marine positions.

Scores of miscellaneous land personnel, in their torn and dirty greens, their faces showing the strain of the fighting which had been going on for more than two months, trooped around to shake Commander Montgomery's hand, or simply to wave at him. At the moment, the four boats of Squadron Three seemed to be the defending navy of Guadalcanal.

When Montgomery got back to the new squadron office on Tulagi, he found that someone had nailed the squadron insignia over the doorway. It was a Disney cartoon figure of a mosquito lugging a torpedo, a fierce expression on his face. The numeral three indicated the squadron.

The PTs had officially arrived on the scene.

3.

Baptism by Fire

As if in honor of the PT squadron's arrival, there was no visit by the Tokyo Express on the night of October 12. However, within the next twenty-four hours, one of the biggest and most important of PT night actions was in store for Montgomery's boys.

From patrol planes and secret coastwatchers, who lived under cover among the enemy from Guadalcanal to Bougainville, there was information that three Japanese destroyers, or possibly a cruiser and two destroyers, had been spotted coming down The Slot toward Guadalcanal. Commander Montgomery, with the supreme confidence that goes with good morale and a new weapon, went to General Rupertus to ask

if the General felt that the PT fleet should be
risked against so inconsiderable a target as a
Japanese cruiser and two destroyers.

General Rupertus, a battle-wise marine, was
aware of the fact that miraculous new and un-
tested weapons, such as the PTs were at that
moment, had a way of falling short of expecta-
tions in the utter confusion and unimagined
emergencies of battle. He also knew that the
intelligence reports passed on by coastwatchers
and patrol planes were frequently inaccurate,
and often they erred on the conservative side.
Instead of a cruiser and two destroyers, as reported, the Japanese force could be battleships,
heavy cruisers and a fleet of destroyers.

General Rupertus also knew that, aside from
a few auxiliary vessels lightly armed with 20-
millimeter deck guns, and the old destroyers
protecting cargo ships unloading on the Guadalcanal side, there was virtually no defending
navy in the vicinity. Nevertheless he didn't
want to disturb Commander Montgomery's
esprit de corps, so he agreed with Montgomery
that the Japanese force didn't sound too formi-

dable, and he advised the PT commander to keep his boats prepared for action.

Montgomery went back to squadron head-quarters to make sure his boats were ready to go. There were a thousand details to be checked before he could at last lie down to get some sleep.

At 2:00 A.M., on the morning of October 14, he was awakened by the powerful voices of big guns booming from the direction of Guadal-canal. Flashes of white light flickered across the southern sky. Two Japanese battleships were opening a terrific shelling of Henderson Field with their gun batteries. High-explosive shells, fourteen inches in diameter and just short of five feet long, were screaming toward the run-ways and revetments of the airfield. This night was to go down in Marine history as "The Bom-bardment."

Within a few minutes the PTs left their base at medium throttle, heading to the south against an unknown naval force in the dark. At first the four boats maintained radio con-tact as they charged across the black waters.

Then, suddenly, the greenish-yellow light from the bombardment of Henderson Field illuminated the water and the four PT boats with all the clarity of a flash bulb. Almost immediately, shells smashed through the air around them and, amid screeching sounds, white geysers of water shot up from the boats. At once the boats separated and, in the excitement, lost radio contact.

Now, sharp white prongs of light from Japanese searchlights swept the water. One caught PT-48 in a blinding illumination. The PTs had contacted the Japanese destroyer screen. The Japanese destroyer crews, by this time experts in night warfare, rapidly illuminated the scene with star shells, which shot flares high up in the sky. Then they let the PTs have the benefit of their 4.7-inch guns.

In the hurly-burly of the engagement, most of the PTs managed to fire torpedoes. On Lieutenant Robert Searles' Boat Number 38, two torpedoes stuck in their tubes, sending out showers of sparks and thumping and crashing like automobiles with blown-out engines. The boat dodged away at top speed, the dud torpedoes hanging half out of their tubes.

The other two torpedoes swung free of PT-38. The excited crewmen, craning back to watch the Japanese from bouncing decks, thought they saw a hit on what seemed to be a large warship tentatively identified as a cruiser.

Boat Number 48, caught by a Japanese destroyer's searchlight, managed to escape into the darkness after frantic twisting and turning. But she almost rammed a second destroyer in the darkness, and was re-illuminated in searchlight glare. This time, the enemy destroyer was so close that her main batteries of 4.7-inch guns could not be depressed enough to fire on the PT—or perhaps there wasn't time for her gunners to train their weapons. However, the small automatic weapons on the destroyer's deck opened up with everything they had and made the night livid with the sailing red-orange globes of their tracer shells. On the PT boat's deck, the two .50-caliber turrets were quickly trained toward the smoky white eye of the enemy destroyer's searchlight, sweeping it and the high superstructure of the enemy ship with a long burst of fire. The searchlight went out, apparently smashed by the American machine-gun fire, and Boat Number 48 escaped into the darkness.

Meanwhile, Boats Number 46 and Number 60 were hotly engaged with the enemy. PT-60, which carried Commander Montgomery on her bridge and therefore was the squadron flagship, had been slightly ahead of the other PT boats, and she had penetrated farther into the Japanese destroyer screen than the others. Lieutenant Jack Searles, the skipper and a brother of Bob Searles on PT-38, had fired two torpedoes at what appeared to be an enemy-cruiser silhouette. Those were all the torpedoes he had. The other two torpedo tubes had been removed in a last-minute alteration to make room for depth-charge racks.

Having unloaded her major weapons, PT-60 was little more than a sitting duck. Two Japanese destroyers took her under fire with their main batteries. Dodging like an antelope, she streaked away to look for shelter somewhere in

the dark. In maneuvers, Commander Montgomery had learned that one tactic for such an
emergency was to make smoke—to set off the
smoke generators on the boat's stern. As the
pearly clouds poured into the air, a shell
screeched and slammed into the boat's roaring
wake, sluicing her stern with water.

Lieutenant Searles swung the PT back into
her own smoke. The Japanese destroyers, mo-
mentarily frustrated, began firing into the clouds
with 20-millimeter shells. The PT crew could
see the bright-red coals of the tracers sailing
through the smoke. Searles and Montgomery, on
the bridge, tried to set a compass bearing which
would take them to Tulagi. But right behind
them charged one of the destroyers, firing main
battery and automatic weapons with frightening
accuracy. Searles whipped his boat into and out
of its far-spread smoke cloud, trying to maintain
the general direction toward Florida Island and
Tulagi.

Then the smoke generator ran out of fuel. The
protective tail of white dropped away, and the
crewmen of PT-60 had nothing but the shadows

of night to hide them. As the shells screeched by and the red streaks of the 20-millimeter tracers arched over their heads, Commander Montgomery had a last-minute inspiration. He called for the launching of the depth charges, a strange weapon against a ship which had a much stronger hull than the PT herself. But Montgomery, discussing the incident later on, said he was willing to try anything.

Just before the depth charges were rolled overboard, the crewmen tossed the smoke generator over the stern. The depth charges, going off with a muffled concussion, sent up two columns of geyser-like water behind the PT. The destroyer skipper evidently suspected some kind of new weapon and halted his ship. While she nosed around the spot where the smoke generator had fallen, the PT boat gained a lead, making sure progress toward the dark land mass of Florida Island and Tulagi.

Quickly, Montgomery found a small inlet where the boat might take cover. The PT roared up a little arm of a bay, and Searles chopped the engines. The boat lay close to the shore, in the

lee of a steep bank. The crewmen held their
breath, while the fast-moving shape of the destroyer charged past to the seaward, her bow
tracing a wide white comb of foam, her wake
rising phosphorescent behind her long stern. She
failed to see the American foe as she swept by.

Meanwhile, the other three PT boats, their
fighting done, were separately retiring at slow
speed in the direction of Tulagi. Each boat crew
thought theirs was the only PT to survive the
night's dreadful action. By four o'clock the
waters seemed still and the mountainous dark
mass of Guadalcanal to the south no longer
showed flashes of gunfire. With the first rays of
day beginning to lighten the sky, Lieutenant
Robert Wark, on PT-48, decided to see if he
could contact any of his squadron mates by radio.

He was successful in establishing contact
with Number 38 and Number 46, but failed
to reach the squadron flagship carrying Commander Montgomery. PT-60 was still lying in
the lee of Florida Island, and now, when things
seemed to have quieted in the bay, the engines
were slipped into gear. But the boat moved only

slightly. She was grounded on coral rock, caught by the lowering of the tide in her hideaway.

Commander Montgomery opened up with his radio and contacted the squadron base at Tulagi, asking for help. The disconsolate members of the crew of PT-60 were afraid now that their boat was going to be out of action for a while. She was filling with water; the rips in her bottom must be considerable.

Finally, that afternoon, a chubby little YP, a converted tuna-fishing boat from the California coast, chugged into the inlet to assist in prying the PT boat loose and towing her back to base. But it was plain she was seriously, if not mortally, damaged. It would be a long time before she could fight again.

Later that day, the skippers of the four boats hashed over the action, salting down the bitterly learned lessons of the engagement. They could see that they would really have to use their PTs with all the stealth and furtiveness of a jungle cat. They would have to sneak up on the enemy targets as slowly as possible—keeping their engines in gear, but just barely turning over—

approach to a firing range of one thousand yards,
then streak away the second the torpedoes were
fired. If necessary, they must make smoke to
cover their retreat. These were the tactics to be
followed consistently in future night PT boat
operations in the Solomons area.

When the Japanese intelligence reports on
this Squadron Three action were recovered after
the war, it was discovered that there had actually
been no PT hits on any of the vessels in the Japanese bombardment force. Apparently the explosions which the PT crewmen took to be hits were
actually the concussive roaring and bright flash-
ing of the Japanese main batteries.

On the other hand, the Japanese had declared
in their own communiqués that their naval force
had been assaulted by *nineteen* enemy torpedo
boats and had sunk twelve of them. Even among
the veteran Japanese the frantic confusion of a
night action could easily lead to exaggeration. It
was plain that the PTs had had a great psychological effect. In fact credit is usually given to
this PT boat attack for helping to influence the
Japanese to terminate their bombardment when
they did.

In the daylight, the effects of the Japanese bombardment were only too painfully apparent to the Marine defenders of the Guadalcanal beachhead around Henderson Field. More than nine hundred 14-inch shells had raked the field —back and forth, up and down—in expert fire patterns. The day before there had been ninety fighter planes and dive bombers capable of operating out of Henderson Field. Now the revetments were filled with wrecked aircraft, and only forty-two planes remained in flyable condition. The gasoline supply, which had been sparse before, was almost completely burned out by the bombardment. Worse still, the field was now a landscape of moon craters, and the dead and wounded from the tremendous bombardment numbered over a hundred—with forty-one dead.

The situation of the American beachhead on Guadalcanal was extremely grave. The newly arrived PT boat squadron under Commander Montgomery was in sad shape, too, with half of its strength—two boats—out of action. PT-60 seemed to have suffered almost irreparable damage from her enforced beaching on coral rocks, and the crew of PT-38 were still trying to repair the damage caused by the two defective torpedoes. But at least, in their baptism of fire, the PT crews had learned fast and developed methods that would be useful during the months of heavy fighting which were to follow in the Solomons.

4.

On the Way to Action

While the fighting was raging around the Solomon Islands, Ensign John F. Kennedy's service history was slowly developing in the United States. On September 27, 1942, he reported for duty at the PT training school at Melville and started tackling the strenuous course of instruction which was to qualify him as a PT boat skipper.

Melville, now in its eighth month of operation, had come a long way since it was founded in a few Quonset huts on a mud flat. It had become a highly active training center with a long line of Quonset huts for the officers and a sizable barracks for the enlisted men. The boats of 'Ron Four, the training squadron, were mostly old

Elco 77-footers, but a new 80-footer, PT-114—one of the same batch as PT-109—had been added to the fleet. All of these boats, of course, were kept in faultless condition, as is fitting for equipment in a military training school.

There were lines of large Quonset huts for classrooms, machine shops and mess halls. The training included regular classes and instruction periods in navigation, communications, engineering and gunnery. The gunnery classroom work was confined to the recognition of friendly and enemy planes and ships, and the stripping and assembling of weapons. In addition, there was instruction in the engineering and care of torpedoes.

The concentrated period of classroom cramming was accompanied by regular physical training workouts—setting up exercises, judo and an obstacle course—to increase the trainees' physical tone, so they could take the drubbing they would have to endure in the bouncing PT boats. After this part of the work was completed, the students moved on to boat training.

The course was about two months long and

there were three grades of intensity of instruction in the classroom work: A, B and C. Every student had to pick some specialty, such as engineering, navigation and seamanship, gunnery, or radio and flag signaling. In his specialty, the individual must take the intensive grade (A) and he could choose the A, B or C course in the other subjects. But every crewman had to have a rounded education in all the different skills of the PT boat.

Officers were required to take at least the B course in all of their subjects. The program objective of "Specht Tech" (this nickname was derived from the name of Commander W. C. Specht, who set up the course) was to train 2,500 officers and 15,000 men for operating a torpedo squadron force wherever needed. It would produce more than a thousand crews if the war lasted that long, and if PT boats continued to be in demand as the world-wide struggle continued. The PT force was a long way from that objective now, since Elco was still building boats with numbers in the early hundred bracket. And the Higgins Company in New Orleans, which had mass-produced the vast majority of landing boats used in amphibious operations all over the world, had just started constructing its version of the PT boat.

Knowing John Kennedy's record for concentration on a subject when he was eager to tackle it, we could have predicted that he would study the A course in all of his subjects—and he did. His best subject was navigation and seamanship. This probably stemmed from the fact that Kennedy had practically grown up on small boats. Commander Edward J. Farley, one of the founding fathers of the Melville school wrote: "A few trainees knew small boats well. They were quick to catch on."

But all of the enlisted men and officers at Melville were volunteers, and therefore they were much more eager to do well than the ordinary draftees. John Kennedy did extremely well. The squadron boats practiced maneuvers in the bleak, stormy and, at this time of year, icy cold waters of Narragansett Bay on the south shore of Massachusetts. From the family home at Hyannis Port, Kennedy had ranged in small boats through many of the same stretches of water in which the PT crews now maneuvered. So he was in a very familiar environment. When he graduated and was given his "PT Boat Driver" rating, he had done so well that he was ordered to stay on as an instructor in the school.

For many a young graduate this would have been a desirable berth. Kennedy, who had been promoted to the rank of lieutenant (junior grade) shortly after his arrival at Melville, might well have thought he was in an ideal spot. He was living in the neat confines of the school, not too far from several of the larger New England cities, and above all only a short distance away from his family's home at Hyannis Port.

But the Lieutenant was eager to be on his way to a battle front. He was familiar with the brave exploits of the first PT heroes in the Philippines, and he wanted to get a Pacific assignment and join the fight. But at Melville, as in his Washington job, he had to buck the inertia that seems always to be present in a large military establishment. For weeks and months Kennedy remained there as an instructor, meanwhile trying every possible means of getting himself assigned to overseas duty.

In his time at Melville Kennedy was apparently a very effective instructor. He worked hard at his job, despite the fact that he was restive and eager to get out to one of the battle fronts. He also made some lifelong friends. One of these was a student of his, Paul B. Fay, Jr.

During his first days at Melville, Fay was playing touch football with a group of officers. In the course of the game he got into a violent argument about the rules with a very youthful man who didn't seem to be much older than a high school student, to judge from appearances. The young man turned out to be John Kennedy, but at that point Fay didn't know Kennedy by name, nor did he have the slightest inkling that Kennedy was an instructor.

The next day Fay was ordered to report aboard one of the squadron boats for maneuvers in the bay area. The boat he was assigned to was one of the old 77-footers, but instead of carrying out orders, he smuggled himself aboard the new 80-foot Elco. After the maneuvers, he was ordered to report immediately to the squadron instructor, a Lieutenant (j.g.) Kennedy. Kennedy fixed him with an icy stare and said, as Fay recollected the conversation later on: "Listen, Fay, if every officer made his own rules in this Navy, the Japs would lick us in a week. I could have you thrown out of motor torpedo boats for what you did this afternoon, and if you disobey orders again, I will."

These were strange beginnings for a close friendship, but later, when both Fay and Kennedy were working out of the Tulagi base as PT commanders, the two men became close friends. And eventually, when John F. Kennedy became President of the United States, Paul B. Fay, Jr. was appointed Undersecretary of the Navy.

After tedious months of duty as a PT instructor, Kennedy's efforts to get a battle-front assignment at last bore fruit. In February of 1943 he received orders to proceed to Motor Torpedo Boat Squadron Two for assignment. This, of course, meant an ocean voyage to the Solomon Islands area, for Kennedy's orders were of the

low-priority type. After all, he was a very junior
officer going out as a replacement, and he had to
pick his way to the Pacific by "first available
transportation," including slow steamship where
necessary.

It was March before Lieutenant Kennedy
found his way to San Diego, California. At San
Diego, he earnestly sought air or sea transport—
the rapid kind; but with a low-grade priority his
passage was slow in coming. He finally managed
to get aboard a former French passenger liner,
renamed the U.S.S. *Rochambeau,* and pressed
into service in the Pacific as a United States
troop transport. The trip through the Equato-
rial waters and across the vast blue magnificence
of the South Pacific—Kennedy's first venture
into the world's largest ocean—might have been
pleasurable if the young lieutenant had not been
in such a hurry to get to the front and into the
fight.

5.

The Tide Turns on Guadalcanal

At the torpedo boat base on Tulagi, the PT skippers were rapidly becoming professional fighters. The second section of Squadron Three had joined the first four boats, and on moonlit nights they patrolled, searching for enemy landing craft scuttling along the Guadalcanal shore. They shot up the shadowy barges when they could or, finding none, they smashed the quiet of Cape Esperance by blasting with all their guns at any enemy movement they could see.

But on the moonless nights—then they had to look out for the *big* trouble. For on those dark nights their job was to stop the Tokyo Express. Usually the PT headquarters received early warnings from coastwatchers up The Slot and from patrol planes searching during the daylight hours. In this way they generally had an approximate idea of the enemy's strength, though it was seldom entirely accurate.

Hugging the dark masses of the islands so that they wouldn't be visible, the fleet of PTs would creep into position as the enemy approached. The usual technique was to edge in toward the enemy until they reached a range of a thousand yards. Then they fired torpedoes, two at a time, with enough spread so that an enemy destroyer would be bracketed. At a thousand yards, that spread of two degrees was just about the length of an enemy destroyer, and the chances of a hit were much greater.

The main objective was concealment: the stealthy approach, the sudden shot from the dark; then the rapid retreat, with evasive dodging maneuvers and emission of smoke clouds to cover the movement. These were the tactics learned so forcibly on the first night of action, October 14.

In late November, 1942, another PT squadron arrived at Tulagi to reinforce Montgomery's badly shot-up Squadron Three. This was Squadron Two, which was composed in part of squadrons and boats first put into service at the Brooklyn Navy Yard and then sent to the Panama Canal Zone for further training. Among the mixture of old 77-foot boats and the latest 80-footers were included PT-59 and PT-109, both destined to play an important part in Lieutenant John F. Kennedy's battle history.

PT-59, under Ensign David Levy, actually did double duty. On alternate nights it was operated by Lieutenant Jack Searles and his crew. Searles' original boat, which had been beached on the coral rock of Florida Island on October 14, was as yet inoperable. In Searles' hands, PT-59 became one of the most famous of the little fighting vessels based at Tulagi.

Gradually the Japanese stopped assigning heavy warships to the job of escorting transports and reinforcements into enemy bases on Guadalcanal. Accordingly the forces which PT Squadrons Two and Three faced were lighter. But even so the Japanese ships were generally destroyers—many times the match of the PTs in speed and power. The Japanese officer in charge of these reinforcing movements was usually the dynamic, dashing little Rear Admiral Raizo Tanaka.

On November 30, Tanaka took a destroyer force in to Guadalcanal with reinforcements and supplies for the Japanese. The PTs were alerted. But this time American Task Force 67—composed of heavy cruisers and destroyers under Rear Admiral Carleton H. Wright—sped to meet the Japanese, and the mosquito boats were not called into action.

In the furious night battle, Tanaka's nine destroyers engaged a superior force of five American cruisers and six destroyers, wreaking havoc on the American ships with expert use of torpedoes. He severely damaged the *New Orleans, Minneapolis* and *Pensacola,* and sank the heavy cruiser *Northampton.* Only one cruiser, the *Honolulu,* escaped damage. The Japanese force lost only one destroyer.

In that action, subsequently called The Battle of Tassafaronga, Tanaka also managed to drop floating drums of supplies off the Tassafaronga

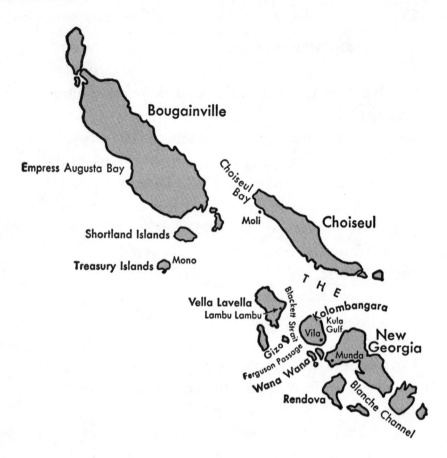

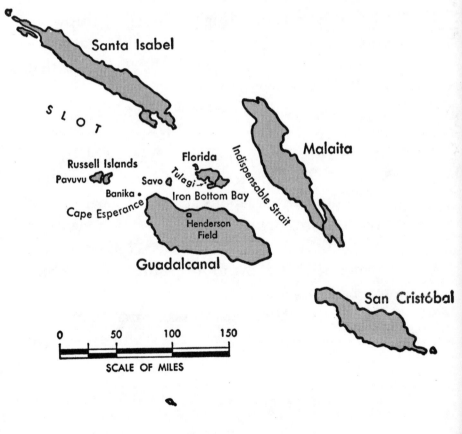

THE
SOLOMON
ISLANDS

N
W — E
S

Santa Isabel

S L O T

Russell Islands
Pavuvu
Banika
Cape Esperance

Florida
Savo
Tulagi
Iron Bottom Bay

Indispensable Strait

Malaita

Henderson
Field

Guadalcanal

San Cristóbal

0   50   100   150
SCALE OF MILES

shore from seven of his destroyers. The drums were safely recovered by Japanese landing barges.

With Task Force 67 out of action, the small fleet of torpedo boats again found itself to be the defending navy of Guadalcanal at night. On December 7, 1942, the first anniversary of the attack on Pearl Harbor, four PT boats went after a fleet of Tanaka destroyers at 11:30 P.M. They flung twelve torpedoes at them and then, amid high-speed maneuvering, managed to throw up enough smoke, spray and .50-caliber and 20-millimeter fire to convince the Japanese that the PT boats were a formidable force.

It was in this engagement that PT-59, captained by Lieutenant (j.g.) John Searles, came within a hundred yards of the Japanese destroyer *Oyashio*. The gunners engaged in a quick duel with automatic weapons as the PT boat snaked away, making smoke. On this occasion even the spunky little Admiral Tanaka was impressed. He abandoned his effort to drop supply drums and reversed his course.

Four days later the Tanaka force again ventured into Guadalcanal waters, this time with ten destroyers loaded with supplies and ammunition. Fourteen SBD Douglas dive bombers from Henderson Field, escorted by fighters, intercepted the force near New Georgia Island. But in the fading daylight they scored no hits with their thousand-pound bombs. So that night, the responsibility fell especially heavily on the mosquito boats. Three PT boats commanded by Lieutenant Les Gamble engaged the Japanese destroyers in Torpedo Junction. As usual they fired torpedoes from dark hiding places along the shore and then streaked away to take cover. Two of the torpedoes from Gamble's force hit the Japanese destroyer *Teruzuki,* leaving her dead in the water and burning brightly.

A new boat of Squadron Two, PT-44 under Lieutenant Frank Freeland, intercepted the radio calls indicating the engagement Gamble's boats had joined. Freeland, eager to get into his first action, rushed over from patrol on Kamimbo Bay. Charging in, he closed on Tanaka's column of destroyers. Silhouetted by flames from the burning *Teruzuki,* the small PT boat was the target for a hail of shells. Swept by searchlights, she quickly retired to the dark. But the irrepressible, if unwise, newcomer charged again at high speed. This time a destroyer leveled a 4.7 turret, fired, and scored a direct hit in the PT's engine room. Then the boat was crushed by heavy salvos from other destroyers as the crew members dived for the water.

The exploding of the boat's gasoline tanks and concussion of the shell explosions killed all but two of the crew. However, the mission of turning back the Tokyo Express had been accomplished, and Gamble's boat had scored a kill on the destroyer *Teruzuki*. The crew of that ship worked valiantly to hold the fires back. But three hours and forty minutes after she had been hit, the flames reached the magazine where her depth charges were kept. She exploded and sank.

The engagement, strangely enough, seemed to discourage the Japanese from forming another Tokyo Express during the rest of December. It became apparent that the PTs were a weapon of psychological as well as physical significance. Even though defended by superior fire power and searchlights, the Japanese destroyers were jittery in the presence of the stealthy, fast-moving mosquito boats.

By this time the veteran PT men were well aware of the failure of some of their equipment to live up to the optimistic predictions of the designers and builders back in the United States. One of the severely limiting factors in achieving the potential of the PTs was poor maintenance. In theory, the PT engines were supposed to be overhauled or replaced every 500 hours, but with the primitive facilities available at Tulagi, this was impossible. The devoted Motor Macs kept the engines going somehow, although there were occasional near-disasters when an engine would quit in the middle of an action. With reduced running efficiency, the speed of the boats was severely cut down.

Another limitation of the efficiency of the boats was the fouling of bottoms and propellers. In the early days at Tulagi, skillful Motor Macs, donning Navy diving suits, went below the water to repair bent screws. By the end of the year, two floating drydocks had been brought up to the

PT base, and the PT tender *Jamestown* had put in to supply mechanical maintenance, torpedoes and a more civilized mess hall than was available on the shore at the PT base facility.

The PT base on Florida Island now was called Calvertville, after Commander Allen P. Calvert, commander of the PT flotilla which had been assembled there. Over the main street of Calvertville hung a sign supported by a bamboo frame: CALVERTVILLE: THRU THESE PORTALS PASS THE BEST M.T.B. FLOTILLA IN THE WORLD. There were thatch-roof lean-tos, tents and sizable mess halls under tenting for the PT men. But the base was still far from civilized. The PT crews, never noted for stern discipline, very often wore only skivvy shorts or dungarees around the camp. And in addition to the oppressive heat, sickness —especially malaria—took a heavy toll.

Besides the nine men killed on Lieutenant Freeland's PT-44, one machinist's mate had died of natural causes; and the original skipper of Squadron Three, Commander Montgomery, and many others had been invalided out with fever. Five of the boats had been damaged by going aground, and two in collisions. However, considering the number of patrols and dangerous engagements, the losses of the PT flotilla had been remarkably low.

A few days before Christmas, 1942, boats of a third squadron arrived on Tulagi to reinforce the splinter fleet. They were the boats of Squadron Six—new 80-foot Elcos. Like half the boats of Squadron Two, the new PTs were a little longer than the older boats, heavier and more comfortable. They were also slightly better insulated around the cockpit with armor plate, though even there the protection was barely sufficient to turn a .25-caliber Japanese rifle bullet. The designers didn't want to burden the boats with too much weight, for fear of impairing maneuverability and speed.

The new squadron was a boost to the morale of the tired veterans of the PT flotilla in Tulagi. Within three weeks, its members went into action.

The night of February 1-2 marked the last big Japanese naval action in the Guadalcanal area.

On the day before this final engagement, ominous tidings began to ripple the air around Calvertville. Coastwatchers and air scouts reported that at least twenty Japanese destroyers, and possibly some cruisers, were heading for Guadalcanal. And all evidence indicated that once again the little PT boats would be the defending navy of Guadalcanal.

Before the sun went down that day, the PT skippers checked into the radio shack for a quick, final briefing. Then at 9:30 P.M. eleven mosquito boats crept along the black, slick stretch of water off Cape Esperance, waiting. It was a pea-soup night with rushing, heavy clouds and a flickering of lightning across the thick, high sky. As the boats inched across Torpedo Junction in a sprawling, loose pattern, all lookouts studied the murky horizon for sudden-looming masses of Japanese ships.

The first two boats to make contact were Les Gamble's PT-48 and John Clagett's PT-111. The contact was at 11:15 P.M. Both PT skippers changed course and inched along a path which would bring them as rapidly as possible, without stirring up a wake, to within a thousand yards of the enemy ships.

Clagett was the first to break the silence. He fired all four torpedoes in a few seconds, the dynamite-primer charge flaring orange in the night. Then he jammed throttles full forward, chopped mufflers, and flung his skittering PT into a spray-plumed turn.

But the Japanese destroyer he was firing at had spotted him, and her shells screeched through the air around PT-111. Sudden white shell splashes plopped on both sides of the boat: fifteen splashes, twenty. Then a shell smashed directly into the paper-thin hull, exploding into a sheet of torchlike flame. The crew slid into the water to escape the burning inferno.

Farther to the west, Gamble was going through the same ordeal: creeping in, holding fire—because every yard gained in the approach to torpedo range could be precious. At nine hundred yards, Gamble stabbed the two lowest torpedo buttons on the dashboard with a punching finger. The "fish" rasped in the tubes, a flash of orange light hit the deck. First two away!

Gamble punched the last two buttons. Two more torpedoes blasted out, slithering into the water.

And now, the retreat!

Again, as with Clagett, the enemy spotted the torpedo boat immediately. The Japanese main batteries flashed, blinked, flashed white in the night. Their screeching shells came, ripping the air; their guns thundered; and a white search-light beam fell instantly across the water, covering all of it at once as it moved about.

"Make smoke!" The black jet of chemical *whooshed* from the generator on the PT's stern. Luminescent clouds of camouflage rolled off the water. Gamble circled in his smoke, trying to nudge toward Savo Island, away from the Japanese destroyer that was charging directly for him. He held his boat straight toward the beach at speed, and she came up hard on the sand. The Japanese destroyers fired a tremendous volley of shots after her. Gamble ordered the crewmen overboard and ashore, on the double. The destroyers could still pulverize the PT with their fire.

Near by, PT-115 was caught in a similar trap. Her skipper made the same decision to beach on the west shore of Savo. Farther south, off Cape Esperance, PT-37 moved into position. As the swift-moving hulk of a Japanese ship came into range, Ensign James M. Kelly fired one, two, three, four torpedoes. The small boat was spotted almost instantly, and again the Japanese were lucky: a direct hit. PT-37 blew up like a giant firecracker, the orange flash painting the sky high up. Only one crew member survived.

But the PT boats in their picket formation, waiting farther down the line for the Japanese onslaught, were far from finished. Closer toward Cape Esperance two of the still splendid new Squadron Six boats, PT-123 and PT-124, waited, and a new kind of engagement developed. A rattling Japanese patrol plane hovered overhead, then dropped a flickering flare and illuminated the boats. The PT skippers had learned that to be illuminated by the lemon-colored, searchlight glare of the flares was not actually to be as naked as they felt. They knew that often the enemy, overhead, couldn't see them even when their boats seemed to be fully illuminated. The PTs waited, hoping that their barely moving dark shapes would not be spotted by the seaplane churning around above.

While they waited, the high dark mass of a Japanese destroyer moved into a lookout's ken. Lieutenant Faulkner, on PT-124, instantly changed course to intercept, closing to torpedo range. There followed the long anxious wait, the anxious slow progress. Faulkner fired—one, two, three torpedoes—then flung his boat into full-speed retreat, making smoke. PT-123 meanwhile, was making the same kind of deliberate, quiet attack, closing to less than a 700-yard range. Just as she was preparing to fire, the Japanese patrol plane rattled ominously overhead, then swooped in to release a bomb. In a freak shot, the "egg" landed straight on the stern of PT-123, ripping it apart in smashing explosion and fire. Four men were flung to death; the rest were recovered next day.

Still more mosquito boats got in their punches only to be surrounded by the jutting shapes of enemy destroyers coming from not one, but several, directions. The simple fact this night was that there were enough Japanese destroyers to enable two or three of them to strike off and mop up opposition, while the bulk of the destroyer line proceeded on its main mission.

Across the slick blackness of Torpedo Junction, flickering orange fires told the story of the valiant attacks made by the PTs. One bright fire marked the burning Japanese destroyer *Makigumo*, which had been driven into an American minefield. The rest were PTs. For the PT flotilla, February 2, 1943, was the saddest day of the Guadalcanal campaign. Three priceless boats were gone for good, and out of the three crews fifteen men were dead or missing. At that moment the PT skippers and crews would probably have said that they had failed, despite the damage they had inflicted. The main body of the Japanese destroyer force was going ahead calmly, arrogantly with its mission, contacting the land forces on the front. Of course, the men from the PTs had no way of knowing that the

mission the Japanese were carrying out successfully was not reinforcement, but evacuation.
The tide had turned.

On February 9, General Alexander M. Patch
announced that Japanese resistance was ended
on Guadalcanal.

6.

A New Skipper for PT-109

On March 28, less than two months after the
Japanese withdrawal from Guadalcanal, Lieutenant John F. Kennedy finally arrived at Espiritu Santo. During the time he had been traveling, the American command had been preparing
for a massive assault on a series of Japanese island
positions in the central Solomons. As the first
step, Admiral Halsey's marines and the 43rd
Division had moved into the Russell Islands—
about half the distance to New Georgia. The
Russell Islands were secured without any resistance. The small enemy garrison of less than 300
Japanese troops had shoved off before the Americans arrived.

Immediately, Navy construction battalions,

the famed Seabees, moved in with their bull-
dozers to build a landing strip in the coconut
groves of one of the Russell Islands, Pavuvu. On
another, called Banika, they set up a subsidiary
PT-boat base, which would serve as a staging
area for the main mosquito boat headquarters
at Tulagi and Florida islands.

On April 7, Kennedy sailed into the Guadalcanal area on an LST (landing ship, tank), which
was carrying a load of cargo and passengers from
Espiritu Santo. The passengers included Army
replacements who were to be landed at Guadalcanal, as well as Navy officers whose destination
was the small island of Tulagi.

Tulagi, the principal naval port of the rapidly
growing Guadalcanal base, had been enjoying a
period of relative peace for several weeks. As a
result, Tulagi Harbor on April 7 was practically
chock-a-block with United States Navy shipping
—cruisers, destroyers, artillery and supply vessels
at anchor.

For the past three days, however, coastwatchers
and scouting planes had been reporting considerable increase in enemy ship and plane movement

behind enemy lines. The reports of the American air scouts indicated that there had been a sudden build-up of aircraft in the Japanese bases scattered through the central and northern Solomons. For instance, 114 planes were presently based at Kahili, on the southern tip of Bougainville, as contrasted with only 40 the day before.

The air commander at Henderson Field ordered maximum readiness in expectation of attack, so that on the morning of April 7, seventy-six fighter planes were ready to fly out from Henderson.

The first warnings of a Japanese sweep toward Tulagi and Guadalcanal came from coastwatchers around Bougainville at about noon. But it wasn't until 2:00 P.M. that the United States radar station in the Russells broadcast a contact report. Their radar showed nearly two hundred blips heading toward Guadalcanal. The actual number was 110 "Zekes"—or Zero—fighters, plus 67 "Val" dive bombers. It was the largest Japanese aerial attack since the assault on Pearl Harbor on December 7, 1941, and the Guadalcanal radio made an unprecedented broadcast. The usual warning of "Condition Red" was changed to "Condition Very Red."

As the LST carrying Lieutenant Kennedy approached the island of Guadalcanal, she intercepted the radio warning of "Condition Very Red." The ship increased her speed to the maximum and headed for the protective cover of a group of destroyers. Her cargo included a load of bombs, which would endanger the safety of both the crew and the ship in the event of a direct strike by Japanese aircraft. Some of the passengers of the LST gathered on the high stern deck and scanned the sky anxiously.

Snub-nosed blue Grumman fighters began to buzz over the LST as they rose from Henderson Field to meet the expected Japanese raid. The crowd on the deck of the LST watched the fighters streak toward Tulagi, the island hidden in the mist across the bay. There, the fighter pilots knew, were the prize targets of any Japanese air raid—tenders, tankers, auxiliary vessels and landing ships.

Fortunately the big cruisers—the *Honolulu,*

Helena and *St. Louis*—were not in Tulagi Harbor, but there were still plenty of acceptable targets. Fifteen camouflaged PT boats were clustered along one bank of Florida Island at Calvertville, beside their fat tender *Niagara*. Near by was a big-bellied Navy tanker, the *Kanawha*, which at that moment was getting ready to depart after having dumped a load of fuel for the PTs. And there was a whole fleet of transport ships which had come to the area mainly to deposit troops and supplies on Guadalcanal for later staging areas to the westward. Besides these there were eight or nine miscellaneous auxiliary vessels—tenders, a mine sweeper, an old New Zealand auxiliary, a former coaster, called *Awahou.*

On the Guadalcanal side there was also a considerable number of ships. Off Lunga lay the U.S.S. *Tappahannock.* She had been discharging aviation gasoline for the aircraft at Henderson Field. Near her was an escorting destroyer, the *Woodworth,* and again, as on the Tulagi side, a fleet of transports, supply ships and auxiliaries, with destroyers escorting them. One of these destroyers was the *Aaron Ward*. As the clangor of Condition Red rang across the Lunga waters, a pocketful of auxiliary vessels, tugs and other small craft made for the destroyer's side like chicks. They were seeking shelter under the wings of her anti-aircraft batteries. The skipper of Kennedy's LST began to circle, making the ship less of a target for enemy bombers.

One of the prime targets of the Japanese raid was the tanker *Kanawha*. Shortly after three o'clock she was falling in beside a destroyer and a wooden patrol craft when about fifty enemy planes were sighted coming in toward Tulagi from the direction of Savo Island. Nearly half of these headed straight for the *Kanawha*, a tempting, 14,500-ton target. Almost immediately, ten or fifteen Japanese Val dive bombers swooped in on her. Observers from the shore saw the ballooning geysers of bomb splashes leaping up on both sides of the waddling tanker. Then a rolling cloud of smoke with streaks of flame burst across the deck.

On the Guadalcanal side, the attacking fleet of Vals hit the destroyer *Aaron Ward*. By this

time, Lieutenant Kennedy had joined the other
passengers on the deck of the LST, and from
there he could see the planes diving, the ack-ack
splattering the sky. While the group watched,
one enemy bomb scored a direct hit on the
Aaron Ward's engine room; two more went off
alongside. The skipper took damage-control
measures and, when the worst of the air raid
was over, hitched a towline onto a tug with the
objective of reaching Tulagi before sinking. He
didn't quite make it. Five hours later, after a
laborious tow across Iron Bottom Bay and heroic
salvage efforts of crew and officers, the destroyer
went down three miles short of Tulagi. (The
body of water bounded by Guadalcanal on the
south, Savo Island on the west, and Tulagi and
Florida islands to the north became known as
Iron Bottom Bay because of the staggering ton-
nage of Japanese and American warships that
found their final resting place in those black
depths.)

Several of the Japanese bombs landed close
enough to Kennedy's LST to spray the lumber-
ing landing craft with water, but fortunately

none of them made a direct hit. Grumman
Wildcats out of Henderson Field cut arcs in the
sky, chasing Japanese Vals and tangling with
Zero fighter planes. American fighter pilots and
ack-ack gunners claimed they had shot down
more than a hundred enemy planes on that frantic afternoon. The more modest report from
intelligence confirmed a score of twelve Val
bombers, twenty-seven Zekes. United States
losses were confined to seven Marine fighter
planes; all but one of the pilots were rescued.

Everything on the water that afternoon was
firing furiously, including the tugs and LSTs.
But for Lieutenant Kennedy the real drama of
that first day of life in the Solomons was the fighting overhead. He experienced the anxiety of a
first air raid, and for the first time he saw men
dying.

The Japanese attack delayed Kennedy's arrival at Tulagi by several days. For the skipper
of the LST, fearful of a follow-up enemy raid,
withdrew temporarily from the area. It was
April 12 before the ship finally arrived at
Guadalcanal. And shortly after, Lieutenant Ken-

nedy eagerly reported for assignment to Commander Calvert, the PT-flotilla leader at Tulagi and Florida islands.

As it turned out, Kennedy was given his own command in less than three weeks. While he waited, he was allowed to roam around the base, become familiar with the squadron headquarters, the radio call signs and the maintenance of the boats at the overstrained floating dry-dock. He enjoyed hanging around the headquarters shack, listening to the conversation of the experienced PT crews.

When assigned as a replacement to the PT flotilla headquarters, Kennedy had been given to understand that there was an urgent need for new crews and commanders. But once on the scene, he found that every job seemed to be taken. In fact, the PT flotilla based at Tulagi and Florida islands now had more than 400 officers and men in its ranks. There were crews standing by, waiting their turn to take the boats out on alternate nights.

In the uneasy calm after the Japanese evacuation of Guadalcanal, the remaining boats of the three initial PT squadrons had been divided again, this time into Squadrons Two and Three. The remnants of Squadron Six—the last of the PT squadrons to appear at Tulagi before the end of the Guadalcanal campaign—were split up. A few of the boats were sent on to General MacArthur's command in New Guinea, where there was a continuing demand for the swift, light craft, to be used as gunboats for harassing the Japanese landing boats. The others were assigned to Squadrons Two and Three.

Then, at last, two more new squadrons, Five and Nine, were brought into the Tulagi flotilla headquarters. So now there were four squadrons operating between Tulagi and the recently established base on Banika Island in the Russells. As the large amphibious force shaped up for the assault in the New Georgia Islands, between thirty and thirty-five PT boats were available for battle duty.

However, the PT base at Tulagi, and even the advance staging base at Banika in the Russells, were now too far removed for nightly forays into Japanese territory. Such patrols as were run were usually undramatic scouting expeditions around the shores of the American-occupied Russell Islands. The PT boats were on the lookout for any distant Japanese landing-craft movements along the shores of the New Georgia island group to the west. Lieutenant Kennedy managed to get himself assigned temporarily as a relief executive officer in a couple such routine patrols during the early part of April. But no enemy was sighted.

Then, toward the end of April, the young lieutenant was assigned a boat of his own—the veteran PT-109. By an odd coincidence, he was relieving as skipper the very man who had first been assigned to the craft when it was fresh from the factory—Bryant L. Larson. Though Larson had had other assignments in the meantime, he was now back with PT-109 and ready for a rest after his strenuous tour of duty.

Though PT-109 was one of the first group of 80-footers to be built by the Elco works, she was still one of the most recent models to be added to the Calvertville flotilla. She was equipped with self-sealing gas tanks and bunks for a crew of eleven. And despite her battle scars, earned during the Guadalcanal campaign, the grimy veteran craft still seemed like a personal present from the United States government to the young naval officer who was to command.

But Kennedy was already a responsible leader. He had learned that a good PT crew sticks together—enlisted men and officers alike. They look after each other and have a group responsibility in their boat. He was lucky in being provided by headquarters with an excellent crew. Most were veterans of considerable service, graduates of Melville, and they came from many other squadrons. The executive officer was Ensign Leonard Jay Thom, of the original veteran outfit, 'Ron Two. Lenny Thom was well over six feet tall, broad-shouldered, muscular. To add an extra picturesque note to his thatch of blond hair, he had grown a pointed goatee beard which carried threads of white. He was big, jovial, outgoing.

The enlisted men were assigned as follows. Andrew Jackson Kirksey, the torpedoman (2/c), was guardian of the splinter boat's big

punch. His was the skilled job of keeping the
motors and gyros, impellers and propellers of
the torpedoes in impeccable order. Every time
the PT boat loaded up to do battle, he superin-
tended the work of heaving the torpedoes into
their torpedo tubes from the storerooms of the
tender *Niagara*. His battle station was next to
the rear torpedo tube on the port side, which
was generally the first of the tubes to discharge
its burden in an attack. His job was to watch
and respond to the visual signal given by the
skipper, who raised an arm each time he hit a
torpedo discharge button on the dashboard. Immediately upon the signal, Kirksey snatched up
a maul or mallet and whacked the firing pin on
top of the torpedo tube. This was to double-
check the electrical circuit which was supposed
to fire the tin fish from the tube. The blow would
set off the powder charge by mechanical means,
thus making sure the torpedo would be shot
from the tube in case the electrical activation
hadn't worked.

Communications were of vital importance
too, and the pressure of the radioman's job never

let up. John Edward Maguire carried it by himself. He alone was responsible for passing on contact reports from the flotilla control center, instructions from element leaders and information from other boats on patrol.

When there was contact with enemy landing barges, or when the boat was close enough to engage the deck guns of a destroyer, the two gunner's mates, Charles A. Harris and Maurice Kowal, went to work. And then there was a quartermaster (the Navy term for steersman), Edgar E. Mauer, who manned the wheel when the skipper himself was not steering the boat.

Leon Drawdy and Edmund Drewitch were motor machinist's mates, and theirs was the difficult job of maintaining the three 1350-horsepower aero engines in workable pitch. Later on, two other motor machinist's mates (2/c), William N. Johnston and Patrick Henry McMahon, were added to the crew.

In accordance with the PT tradition, each of the crew members was somewhat grounded in the duties of the others. If anyone were hurt or killed in action, a boat mate could fill in. Each of the officers was also well grounded in each of the specialties. There were some important collateral duties which several of the crew were expected to carry out on many missions. The quartermaster had the important side job of cook, and was expected to provide meals for the crew from the very limited food supplies then available at Tulagi. Almost all of the crew members were required to keep up their gunnery, so that in the event of contact with a hard-fighting Japanese landing craft, or enemy destroyer within machine-gun range, the little splinter boat could give a good aggressive account of herself.

During the first few weeks of patrol duty, PT-109 was involved in no fighting, nor did she have any contact at all with the enemy. Nevertheless, the patrols were long and arduous and taxing. Maneuvering the 80-foot delicate speedboat amid coral reefs, shoals and sandbars, on moonless nights, was a trick to tax the seamanship of the best boat handlers. And it was always vital to be on the alert for surprise attack at any moment. One never knew where the enemy might suddenly strike, or from what direction. The long, exhausting hours of the patrols took their toll in physical fatigue—especially when coupled with the primitive living conditions.

In the course of these patrols Lieutenant John F. Kennedy was undergoing the long processing of boredom and surprise, shock and injury, humor and irony, courage and dedication, which would make him a veteran.

Late in May, Kennedy and PT-109 were sent up to the advance base on the Russell Islands as part of Squadron Two under Commander Alvin Cluster. Cluster was an Academy man with a vast experience in PTs. He had started in the pre-war days when the first Squadron Two was working out basic doctrine around the Brooklyn Navy Yard. In the very early stages of the Pacific War, Cluster had taken a PT squadron down to Funafuti, east of the Solomon Islands. Then he had been assigned to take over the command of the newly regrouped Squadrons Two and Three at Tulagi and the staging base in the Russell Islands. In taking over this command, he had

moved into a spot vacated by the valiant early
pioneers of PT warfare in Tulagi base: Alan
Montgomery, the Searles brothers, Tom Kendall, Les Gamble and the other veterans who had
withstood the first shocks of combat with the Japanese in the Solomons waters. Most of these pioneers had been sent back to the States for rest and
recuperation.

Strangely enough, Cluster still had most of the
original Squadron Two and Three boats. It was
only Squadron Six, the last of the early groups
to come in before the end of 1942, which had
suffered severe casualties and attrition. Some of
the remaining original Squadron Six boats had
been sent to New Guinea, but the rest were left
to reinforce Squadrons Two and Three.

One of the original Squadron Two boats, of
course, was PT-109. Before the end of the summer, this battle-scarred veteran—as well as her
skipper and crew—were destined to participate
in what was to become one of the most famous
PT-boat actions of World War II.

7.

PT-109 Goes into Action

Toward the end of June, 1943, there were rumors that the invasion of New Georgia might start at any moment. The PT skippers understood that one of the first objectives of the invasion would be the seizure of the island of Rendova, the southernmost of the New Georgia group. And if a PT base were set up on Rendova, the little mosquito boats would be within close striking range of the whole New Georgia island group.

At the principal PT base at Tulagi, Commander Calvert shepherded his strength for the next forward move. On the eve of the New Georgia invasion, he could count on four squadrons. The plan was to move advance elements

of Squadron Nine (six boats), under Lieutenant
Commander Robert Kelly, into Rendova imme-
diately after the landing, if it were successful.
Bob Kelly had distinguished himself during the
Philippine campaign with Bulkeley's original
Squadron Three, and he had now come up to
Calvertville with some new 80-footers.

Once they were based in Rendova Harbor, the
boats of Squadron Nine would be operating
directly out of New Georgia waters, and striking
deep into Japanese-held territory in these islands. And as the fighting progressed on the
ground, other PT squadrons, such as Squadrons
Two and Three under Commander Cluster,
would shuttle boats in to take their turns. That,
of course, would mean that Kennedy and his
crew in PT-109 would probably get their first
chance to strike at major Japanese naval forces.

On the morning of June 30, 1943, the American invasion armada for New Georgia was in
action before dawn. The main American landing
force, the "Barracudes" of the 172nd Regimental
Combat Team, United States Army, were carried
into Rendova in four transports and two supply

ships, with an escorting convoy of seven destroyers.

The main Japanese positions around Munda air base, on New Georgia, expected a frontal attack on their beaches, and were startled to see that the landing boats from the transports and supply ships were heading instead for Rendova, across the bay. The Japanese had evidently been holding their fire for the expected attack on their own beaches. And it was some time before they gathered their wits and began to lob shells in the direction of the American fleet invading Rendova.

Meanwhile, the bulk of the forces of the combat team had got ashore at Rendova Bay, bowling over the light enemy garrison of less than 300 men. The damage inflicted by the enemy shore batteries firing from Munda was relatively light.

The unloading went miraculously well and at 3:00 P.M.—despite an air raid by twenty-seven Zekes, promptly covered by American fighters —the unloading was finished. Admiral Kelly Turner, in charge of the amphibious operation, ordered retirement of the transport fleet and convoying destroyers.

The Japanese commander at Munda, watching through field glasses the efficient debarkation of American forces at Rendova, characterized the debarkation as "absolutely miraculous." Within two hours after the American ships left, a barrage from heavy 105-millimeter United States Army guns emplaced in Rendova was leveled at the Japanese positions on Munda. For good measure, forty-three American planes from Guadalcanal plastered the Munda airfield with fragmentation bombs.

However, a strike of twenty-five Japanese "Betty," two-engined torpedo planes, covered by twenty-four Zero fighters, reached Rendova that same afternoon. They searched beyond Blanche Channel for the empty American transports returning to home base and found them a few miles to the east, making full speed for Tulagi. A furious battle ensued. Sixteen Corsair fighters from Marine Fighter Squadron 221 jumped on the Bettys and Zeros, while the well-trained anti-aircraft gunners of Admiral Turner's transport fleet opened up on the enemy with everything they had.

But one of the torpedoes dropped by the enemy planes found its mark. It was the only Japanese tin fish to strike one of the ships; and, ironically, it hit the flagship, Admiral Turner's famed *McCawley*. The *McCawley* was struck slightly aft of 'midships, and the engine rooms were flooded. She stopped dead in the water. While damage-control parties struggled to save the ship, Admiral Turner shifted his staff to the destroyer *Farenholt,* and a supply ship took the *McCawley* in tow, with two destroyers detailed as escorts. The remaining ships continued to retire at full speed.

Late that afternoon, at 5:15, eight Japanese dive bombers broke through low clouds and dropped bombs around the *McCawley* and the *Libra,* which was towing the damaged ship. The bombs missed. Three of the dive bombers were shot down by anti-aircraft fire, and the harassed crews of the towship and former flagship believed they had escaped and would possibly make it to Tulagi that night.

Later in the evening, the salvage crew aboard the *McCawley* began to wonder if after all they might lose their struggle. The after compartments had flooded, and the ship was settling by the stern. Shortly after dark, while Admiral Turner, aboard the *Farenholt,* was debating whether to sink the *McCawley,* two torpedo wakes appeared from nowhere in the black water and smashed into her side. She rapidly settled and sank. At first it was believed she had been torpedoed by an enemy submarine.

But the next morning, as Commander Kelly brought his advance elements of PT Squadron Nine into the new base at Rendova, the mystery was solved. Kelly reported that he had sunk a Japanese transport in Blanche Channel. He had been told by the newly established Rendova naval operating base that there would be no friendly ships in the Blanche Channel, and so had assumed that the transport ship was Japanese.

The result of this case of mistaken identity was a strict order by Admiral Turner that the

PTs henceforth would operate under his direct command. He would control their movements through a new liaison officer.

Thus Kelly's error unfortunately resulted in a severe setback for the projected PT operation, which had promised to open up new fields of endeavor for the splinter boats. Because of the disaster, all the other crews, including Kennedy's, were slowed down in their ambition to get at the enemy. And during the bitter battles of Kula Gulf and Kolombangara, fought while American troops were struggling to maintain a foothold in New Georgia itself, the PT squadrons were given orders to stay out of the way of the big ships.

During this "layoff" period, a new commanding officer came to take over the Rendova mosquito boat base. He was Commander Thomas G. Warfield, skipper of Squadron Ten, who had brought the new boats of 'Ron Ten to Rendova with some difficulty. One of the tankers carrying four of the 'Ron Ten boats had been sunk off New Caledonia. The boats floated clear and were manned by their crews. But they were somewhat delayed by the mishap.

Warfield, the senior PT officer in the area, finally brought up not only his boats but some boats of Cluster's Squadrons Two and Three as well. The PT flotilla at Rendova was now very impressive, numbering between fifteen and twenty boats. One of the late additions, arriving about the third week in July, was PT-109, Lieutenant (j.g.) Kennedy commanding.

At Rendova, fate seemed to make up somewhat for the action Kennedy and his crew had missed so far. While PT-109 was on patrols along Blanche Channel, and north along the Japanese-held coast of New Georgia, Japanese float planes twice swooped over the small mosquito boat and illuminated her with the brilliant glow of flares.

A new phase of PT operations had begun. The Japanese were placing greater emphasis on barge operations in the central Solomons. With the increased use of armored, metal-hulled diesel-powered landing barges, carrying 100 men or more from one Solomon stronghold to another, the Japanese were also using increasingly close air cover.

The air cover in this new phase of operations was supplied by single- or double-float seaplanes. These planes were equipped with bombs, full loads of machine-gun bullets for strafing, and parachute and floating flares to illuminate the PT boats which the Japanese planes wanted to distract and destroy.

The PTs had previously encountered float planes in occasional bitter battles in the Solomons; for instance, the night of February 1-2 when PT-123 was sunk by a float-plane bomb. But now the mosquito boats were besieged by the aerial marauders practically every night they set out on patrol to look for enemy barges.

Clashes with enemy planes became a standard expectation for a patrol, and the nerves of the PT crews were even more strained than they had been back in the dramatic Guadalcanal days, when the splinter boats did battle with Japanese cruisers and destroyers.

A staff intelligence officer of Admiral Halsey's

headquarters wrote eloquently on the subject, in a high-level report:

> Float planes proved a psychological as well as a material obstacle. PT crews were on tension throughout the patrol, never knowing when the bomb from their unseen foe would fall. Whenever they did make an attack on an enemy barge, they knew for a certainty that their positions were thereby disclosed, and soon they would be attacked by planes against which they believed they had little defense. Some of the PT boys came to the conclusion that instead of sending their pilots to Bali-Bali, Tokyo, or wherever Jap pilots go for operational leave, the Japs gave them a float plane and sent them out after PTs.

Kennedy's crew on PT-109 contacted no barges on their first patrols, although they chased their share of unidentified shadows as they skulked along the dark New Georgia shores. But they did encounter decided float-plane opposition on two horrifying nights.

On one of their first patrols out of the Rendova base, on July 20, the 109 crew were jumped by a float plane as they rumbled along in the midnight black near Japanese-held Gizo Island. PT-109 was traveling in company with boats 163 and 105 when the enemy aircraft dropped a flare, then buzzed out of the sky with stuttering rounds of machine-gun fire. The three PTs opened up with all available guns, throwing up a screen of ack-ack. The enemy shoved off without dropping bombs.

Two hours later, at about 3:00 A.M., the boats were continuing their patrol—without finding any enemy surface traffic—when a float plane dived on them suddenly and came in strafing. The attack was such a surprise that only PT-163 was able to return the fire. A bomb blasted into the water near 109 with the unexpected fury of a summer thunderclap.

The plane disappeared, but Skipper Kennedy saw that the aircraft had made her mark. The boat had been damaged, and two of his crewmen, Kowal and Drawdy, had been ripped by flying bomb fragments. The Skipper checked and found that the injuries—sharp rips in the flesh of a leg and arm—were not fatal. Yet they were bad enough to warrant skilled medical attention. When the patrol finally returned to the Rendova base, the two wounded crewmen had to be sent back to the hospital at Tulagi base. Along with Edmund Drewitch, who had been wounded on an earlier patrol in an accident involving a depth charge, they would see no more service on PT-109.

Back at squadron headquarters, Kennedy picked up three new crew members: Gerald E. Zinser and Harold W. Marney, machinist's mates, and Raymond Albert, seaman first class.

On the night of July 25-26, Kennedy took PT-109 out on patrol again, searching for barges along with five other torpedo boats out of Rendova.

The boats met no barges, but at about the same time as the last bombing attack (3:00 A.M.), they were jumped by a single-float plane which strafed them, and dropped a bomb. This time the attack was such a surprise that none of the boats could return the fire. The enemy plane dived expertly, dropped the bomb twenty yards off the port bow of PT-105, and scooted away.

The bomb didn't damage the 105 boat, but a single flying fragment raked across the bridge and killed the executive officer. No one else was injured on the boat, and no other boat was hit.

Kennedy's boat was traveling some distance from PT-105 during the bombing, but the crew members of 109, after two harrowing float plane engagements and two battle casualties, were beginning to feel considerable nervous strain.

The fighting skipper was unperturbed. He busied himself with plans for building up the armament of PT-109, so that his boat could give a better account of herself on the expected day when she would tangle with the Japanese barges. Perhaps she might even meet up with the swift destroyers of the Tokyo Express, which occasionally ran troops into the Japanese stronghold of Kolombangara.

Kennedy made plans to secure an old single-shot 37-millimeter anti-tank gun for PT-109. Other skippers had done this, obtaining the ancient rubber-tired gun trails from the army

and mounting them on the bows of the PTs.
They were awkward weapons for PTs, and a
chore to mount and load. But if they could be
aimed and fired, they had a terrific wallop—
more than any other PT weapon so far.

On August 1, Commander Warfield received
a top-secret, extra-urgent message from the Navy
base radio station. It was apparently based
on ultra secret intelligence, and warned Warfield that the Japanese were sending in a Tokyo
Express that night. They were also planning a
heavy air raid to destroy the PT base that day.
The raid came—eighteen bombers which
managed, despite camouflage and anti-aircraft
fire, to wreck two boats tied up at the pier. The
bombs missed PT-109, but one PT boat was hit
directly, and wrecked: two men killed, four
wounded.
That day, the PT-109 crew were filled with
apprehension. There were two extra crewmen
—Ensign George H. "Barney" Ross and torpedoman Ray L. Starkey. Kirksey, the regular torpedoman, confided to Starkey that he didn't

think the boat would be coming back from the night's patrol. A Japanese landing force, being transported by enemy destroyers, had been spotted farther up The Slot by coastwatchers. And this time the cruiser and destroyer forces were not available for interception. They had already been too heavily shot up. The PTs—fifteen of them were available for the night's action—were going to have to take over. The prospects for real action were promising.

8.

Disaster at Sea

At dusk, the fifteen PT boats headed north from Rendova toward the new Torpedo Junction, Blackett Strait, at the southern tip of Kolombangara. According to the coastwatchers, air scouts and intelligence, the new Tokyo Express was headed down The Slot. The mission of the four Japanese destroyers, as was learned much later, was to land supplies for their troops at Vila, on the southern tip of Kolombangara. To get there, they were coming down from the north past Vella Lavella and Gizo. And they would have to pass through the narrows called Blackett Strait, on the south side of Kolombangara.

The fifteen PTs from Rendova came up past

the island called Wana Wana to try to blockade Blackett Strait and keep the Japanese force from slipping through to Vila. The small mosquito boats spread themselves, piecemeal, across Blackett Strait in the best position to intercept.

The two closest to the enemy moving southward were PT-159, Lieutenant Henry J. Brantingham commanding, followed by Lieutenant W. F. Liebenow's PT-157. Brantingham, who had radar in his boat—a new thing for the PTs in those days—closed in about midnight to strafe small radar blips which he believed to be landing craft. He was surprised when a sheet of screaming shells started landing all around him. The blips were destroyers! The two PT boats fired six torpedoes without making a hit. Then they dodged away in a smoke screen.

To the north of PT boats 157 and 159 were Lieutenant Kennedy's PT-109 and Lieutenant J. R. Lowrey's 162. But they were far removed from Brantingham in the dark, and lost radio contact. Seeing the prolonged flashes of gunfire, they surmised that the other two boats had been taken under fire by Japanese shore batteries.

They kept on patrolling at slow speed, between Wana Wana and Gizo to the north of Blackett Strait, trying to get word on what had happened.

Meanwhile, the Tokyo Express was streaking toward Blackett Strait, where four more boats were in position. But here only PT-171 —also equipped with radar—made contact. The division commander, Lieutenant Arthur Berndtson, ordered the skipper to shoot all four of his torpedoes while under fire. But all of them missed.

Three more boats, farther to the east, saw the flashes and closed range. They were spotted by the destroyers, which let go with their main batteries, while overhead an enemy float plane dropped a flare and tried to strafe. The boats fired all their torpedoes—twelve—and claimed hits, but they evidently failed to score. The Tokyo Express of four destroyers swept undeterred and undamaged through Blackett Strait.

It seemed to Lieutenant Kennedy on 109 and

Lieutenant Lowrey on 162 that they had missed all the excitement. Both officers knew from the white flashes and heavy cannonading that ship action had been joined. But their own boats had been too far to the north.

As ordered, they kept on patrolling at slow speed. Only one engine on each boat was in gear in order to keep down the wake. Thus the boats would be less visible to the pesky Japanese float planes in the clouds.

From the babble on the short-wave radio, Kennedy couldn't tell what had happened. Had the PTs sunk the enemy or perhaps turned him back? Or had the destroyers slipped through Blackett Strait and—if so—would they be making their exit on the other side of Kolombangara through Kula Gulf? Or was it possible they had reached their destination and might be coming back through Blackett Strait? Any one of those four possibilities could have occurred. Or more enemy forces—cruisers, destroyers, landing barges, planes—might be coming behind them. One thing Lieutenant Kennedy could be sure of: He had been involved in the kind of big engagement he longed for, and still had not fired a shot.

Time was passing, with no fresh gunfire flashes, new flares or thunder from destroyer batteries. The night was quiet. At 2:00 A.M., the boats were creeping up Blackett Strait, having been joined by PT-169, a stray from another division. PT-157 was also near by, though she had not been in contact with them.

Just about 2:30 A.M., as the boats were edging along in the still, black waters, a lookout in Kennedy's boat suddenly cried out: "Ship at two o'clock!"

The ship was the looming, towering shape of the destroyer *Amagiri,* bearing directly down upon Kennedy and his crew. (The force of four Japanese destroyers was steaming back in a column from a successful supply drop at Vila.)

Kennedy and Radioman Maguire, standing side by side in the cockpit, saw the loom of the destroyer over them. Maguire heard Kennedy yell: "Hey—look at this!"

The young skipper hit Maguire on the arm and ordered, "Sound general quarters!"

Maguire shouted: "General quarters! General quarters!" while Kennedy hit the engine-room telegraph lever signaling engines full ahead. He flung the wheel over hard to the right. The bow of the destroyer was looming ahead now like a charging skyscraper. But instead of turning away from the enemy, Kennedy was trying to line up his boat for a torpedo shot, risking it even at such close range. Before he could bring his range estimators to bear, Kennedy saw with alarm that the PT was responding very sluggishly, failing to turn.

Up on the bow, where Starkey and other crew members had rigged the old 37-millimeter fieldpiece, "Barney" Ross was trying valiantly to get the gun into action against the destroyer. He fumbled with a shell, attempting to shove it into the breech.

At that moment, the looming steel shape crashed into the boat with crushing force, charging diagonally into the right side and knocking Kennedy and Maguire flat onto the cockpit deck. The destroyer severed the boat into two angular pieces, chopping off a section which included the starboard engine. Kennedy, flat on his back, saw above him the raked gray stacks of the Japanese destroyer, illuminated by an orange flash. There were the funnels with the upside-down Y-shape he had studied so many times in recognition courses.

Below decks, gasoline exploded around the engine, searing Engineer McMahon on the face and hands as he was knocked against the starboard bulkhead. At practically the same instant, he was flooded by salt water as the rear corner of the boat began to sink, gasoline still burning on the water.

Starkey, who had jumped for his battle station beside the after starboard torpedo, had fallen into the sinking, flaming engine compartment on the port side.

Johnston, another engineer, had been asleep on deck when Maguire gave the general quarters alarm. He saw the flash, the stack of the destroyer passing, and then was suddenly overboard, being turned end over end in the water by the rotating movement of the destroyer's propeller.

Kennedy struggled to his feet in the cock-pit and saw and heard the gasoline burning on the water. His half of the boat was afloat, kept up by watertight compartments, which were undamaged. Maguire, Mauer and Albert, at least, were still aboard with him.

Gasoline, from the part of the boat which had sunk, was burning on the water only a few feet away. Kennedy was afraid the flames might reach the floating section of the hull, so he ordered the crewmen into the water. But the flames moved the other way, and the men climbed back aboard. Kennedy and Maguire, hearing noises in the water, started to swim around, searching for the missing crewmen: Zinser, McMahon, Starkey, Johnston, Harris, Kirksey and Marney. At this point, ensigns Thom and Ross were also unaccounted for.

Suddenly, from the darkness, Harris called: "Mr. Kennedy! Mr. Kennedy! McMahon's burned bad!"

Guided by a light which Mauer was holding on the floating hull, Kennedy swam in the direction of Harris' voice.

Meanwhile, the other survivors were located floating in their kapok life vests on the other side of the boat. Only Kirksey and Marney didn't answer to their names.

Kennedy told McMahon to float on his back. Then, taking him in tow, he headed for the floating section of the PT, about a hundred yards away. In the slight breeze and chop he had hard going. But he got McMahon to the boat, and started back for the others.

He got back to Harris, who complained he had injured his leg. He had banged it against a torpedo tube in the crash. He mumbled that he was water-logged with his heavy shoes and the heavy sweater underneath his life jacket. Kennedy helped him out of his life jacket and held him up while he shed shoes and sweater. Then he helped him back into the kapok jacket and offered to lead him to the floating hull.

Harris found he couldn't kick with his left leg. It had been numbed by the blow against the torpedo tube. He said, "Skipper, I can't swim!"

"Try," Kennedy told him.

"I can't make it."

Kennedy looked at him. "For a man from Boston, you're certainly putting up a great exhibition out here, Harris."

The Lieutenant thereupon took him in tow and guided him toward the boat. It was a struggle; the hulk was drifting away in the wind. Harris tried to kick but his leg gave him trouble. It took a long time for them to get to the boat.

By this time, Thom and Ross had joined the rescue operation, helping to round up the other survivors floating in the dark. Thom had to tow Johnston, who was semi-conscious from inhaling gasoline fumes, all the way to the floating hulk. Ensign Ross swam to Zinser, who was shouting for help. When Ross reached Zinser he discovered what the trouble was. The Machinist's Mate had on not one but two life jackets, and they were binding his arms. Starkey reached the hull under his own power.

A fairly sizable section of the boat had remained afloat. The airtight compartments in the forward part gave it buoyancy, though it tilted to the rear, and to one side. Kennedy counted heads: Thom, Ross, Zinser, Starkey, Mauer, Albert, Maguire and Harris. McMahon and Johnston were both comatose. Johnston was black-and-blue from the propeller wake and sick from swallowing gasoline. McMahon's face and right leg and arm were burned black. The boat's first-aid kit had been lost in the collision.

Kirksey and Marney were still missing. Crew members called out into the black water for them for half an hour, but there was no answer. Kirksey and Marney were gone—probably from the first moment of collision.

The sky was growing light with the dawn, and the little group of crewmen could see that they were deep in Japanese territory. To the northeast rose the high volcanic cone of Kolombangara, a Japanese stronghold where intelligence put the number of enemy at more than 10,000, with reinforcements coming in nearly every night. To the northwest lay Vella Lavella. Gizo, a small enemy-held island with a new military airfield, was to the west. It was so close they could see Japanese planes taking off and landing.

Kennedy said to the men, "What do you want to do if the Japs come out—fight or surrender?"

Somebody wisecracked, "Fight with what?"

Kennedy, always matter-of-fact, took an inventory of available weapons. They had six .45-caliber GI automatics, Kennedy's own sidearm (a .38-caliber revolver), two sheath knives and a pocketknife. It wasn't much of an arsenal to fight with.

"Well," said Kennedy after the inventory, "what do you want to do?"

A crewman quickly replied, "Anything you say, Mr. Kennedy."

"There's nothing in the book about a situation like this," Kennedy said. "Seems to me we're not a military organization any more. Let's just talk this over."

It was an invitation to debate in the New England town-meeting tradition. And the men discussed the question at some length. Though they agreed that they didn't want to surrender, they were unable to work out any definite plan.

Kennedy listened, and came to a decision he was always to remember. His decision was that there had to be a leader or they would not survive. From then on, during the whole episode, he made decisions and gave clear-cut orders.

His first order was for all able-bodied men to get into the water. The hull had been leaking and gurgling. It was settling lower into the water, and the deck space was cramped. His idea was to leave more room on deck for the injured men, McMahon and Johnston. He also wanted to make the men less visible to Japanese lookouts who might be scanning the bay with binoculars—not to mention the planes taking off from Gizo.

Anxiously, the crewmen watched the burning tropical sky for planes—Japanese or American. They cursed the other PTs which had been with them the night before. Why hadn't they sent a rescue boat or plane? The Kennedy crew had no way of knowing that, after the ramming and explosion, PT-109 and her

crew had been written off as lost. The crewmen of the other boats, having witnessed the
collision, told their intelligence officers that no
one could have survived such a catastrophe.
Back at the Rendova base, plans were made to
hold a memorial service for the PT-109 crew.

At about 10:00 A.M., the hulk, which had
been listing even more steeply, heaved and
turned turtle. McMahon and Johnston slid
into the water. The men had to hang onto the
slippery, sharp-edged V-bottom which was just
barely awash.

At that point, Kennedy made another decision. He motioned toward a low, tiny coral
island which seemed about three miles to the
southeast, and probably was too small to be occupied by the Japanese.

"We're going to that small one," he said.
"We'll have to swim for it. Everyone on the
log."

He referred to one of the heavy 2 x 8 tim-
bers which had been tied together to brace the
37-millimeter cannon on the bow. The tim-

bers had come loose in the collision.

The crewmen tied the square battery lantern, wrapped in a spare life jacket, to the floating wood, and also attached a few pairs of heavy shoes. Clinging to their improvised raft, they kicked their feet to make it go in the desired direction.

Then Kennedy made another decision. "I'll take McMahon," he said. Later McMahon recalled that the Skipper had said it as matter-of-factly as if he were discussing the weather.

The Lieutenant told McMahon to turn over on his back. He would float well for he had on an inflated rubber Mae West life preserver, as well as a heavy kapok life jacket. Kennedy took the two top straps of the kapok jacket and tied them together to form a kind of harness, then took the strap between his teeth. Using the breast stroke, he started swimming toward the island, pulling hard, occasionally swallowing water and coughing.

Ensign Lenny Thom took command of the group that followed with the improvised raft. Kennedy's superior swimming ability kept him ahead of that group, even though he was towing McMahon. Every once in a while he would stop for a rest and ask, to keep McMahon's spirits up, "How are you, Mac?" McMahon, though suffering pain from the impact of the salt water on his burned skin, would reply in the affirmative. "Okay, Mr. Kennedy. How about you?" And he tried to kick his feet to help their progress. Sometimes McMahon would ask: "How far do we have to go?" And Kennedy would respond: "We're going good."

After about five hours of this towing, McMahon heard the Lieutenant say, "Pappy, we're going in." They had reached the island and McMahon could hear the sound of waves on the reef.

The two men crawled slowly through the shallow water and across the beach. They were both exhausted, and they had cut their feet badly on the sharp coral. The other swimmers, with their raft, were slower to reach the island.

While McMahon rested, Kennedy set out to scout the island, which was roughly the shape of a circle, about a hundred yards in diameter. It was well studded with coconut trees, but the only coconuts to be seen were the green ones clustered up in the trees. The exhausted skipper would have welcomed a golden-ripe coconut at this point. At least there were no Japanese anywhere.

When the other group of crewmen reached the island with their raft, Kennedy could tell that they had seen some danger. They lay low by the water, keeping silent. They had glimpsed a Japanese landing barge, with a characteristic high-curved bow, putting along close to the island. Kennedy and McMahon hugged the ground too, and the enemy failed to spot any of the Americans.

After this scare, the exhausted crewmen, including Kennedy, flattened out in some bushes for a rest.

9.

Shipwrecked on an Island

While Kennedy rested in the bushes, his active mind kept on working. He was wondering about the tiny island he was on, and the next one beyond it to the eastward. He didn't know the name of either speck of land, but it seemed to him that he recognized them from the charts. He thought that beyond the second island lay Ferguson Passage, the narrow channel which the PTs had for several nights been using as an approach to Blackett Strait.

It occurred to him that if the PT boats were coming through tonight, and if he could stir his tired body to swim to that other island, he might very well be able to flag down one of the

boats. Then he could direct it over to this island to pick up his crew.

At dusk, he got up and put on one of the
soggy pairs of heavy shoes that had been floated
ashore. He wrapped himself in one of the life
vests, tied the .38-caliber revolver around his
neck, and picked up the battery-powered lantern wrapped inside the kapok vest.

As he headed for the water, he said, "If I find
a boat, I'll flash the lantern twice. The password
will be 'Roger,' the answer will be 'Willco.' "

He walked determinedly toward the beach,
feeling dizzy and unsteady and aware, too, that
the old agonizing backache had come back.
Probably the violent wrench of the collision
had reactivated the old football injury. But the
cool of the water seemed to give him strength.
He struck out eastward toward the small neigh-
bor island, and the crewmen watched him go,
wondering if they would ever see him again.
They knew he had taken a hard fall in the collision, and he had been walking around the island as if his back troubled him severely. Also,

he was obviously exhausted by his long lifesaving ordeal after the wreck, and the tremendous workout of towing McMahon to the island.

The skipper looked skinny, and his crewmen weren't aware of his skill as a swimmer or the hidden reserves of will power which could give him the strength of ten in an emergency. Since the collision, he had been in the water for 15½ hours. Yet here he was, swimming again, risking the tricky currents of the Passage and solitary exposure to the voracious sharks and barracuda known to be numerous in the vicinity.

In the increasing darkness, Kennedy reached the small island next to Ferguson Passage. His plan was to work his way along the coral reef around the island, edging toward the Ferguson Passage side. Protected by the stout soles of his heavy shoes, he found that he could tread safely on the sharp, rough coral.

But now, while there was still some light, he was shocked to see a large, dark shape moving near him in the clear water. He splashed hard to frighten the big fish, and blinked his light.

The black shadow disappeared. But the thought of this danger stayed with him.

As he worked his way along the irregular coral barrier, Kennedy stumbled and staggered over the edgy rock. Frequently he fell into holes, barking his shins on the sharp edges. At last he reached the side of the reef toward Ferguson Passage. It was dark now—nine o'clock by his waterproof watch—and the PT boats should soon be appearing in the channel. He must get out there and wait.

Taking off his heavy shoes, he tied them to the life jacket which supported the battery lantern. Then he started out for the deep water where the PTs were in the habit of passing. He floated there, treading water, listening for the faint rumble of PT engines at part-throttle and full-muffler.

But none came. He began to shiver in the night cold. Then, after about an hour's waiting, he saw, far to the west, white lights, flares, and what appeared to be flashes of cannonading, apparently beyond Gizo. He decided that, for once, the PT boats had not come up through Ferguson Passage but had chosen another route to the battle line.

He started back toward the reef again, staggering along the sharp coral in the pitch-black night. After a halting progress over the holes and snags, he set out for the small island which had been his headquarters since the afternoon.

But this time a strong current began to take him north and east, away from the island and his friends. He swam harder, but he was bone-weary and couldn't hold his own against the drift.

Back on the beach of the home island, one of the men standing watch thought he saw a light. Other crewmen, roused from sleep, also thought they saw or heard something. Hoping that Kennedy had contacted a PT boat, they moved into the water toward the island's reef. But they couldn't see any more signs of life out there—only the phosphorescent lights where the waves were breaking and the faint phantoms of night vision multiplied by imagination. They went disconsolately back to shore, convinced that what they had seen and heard was some nightmarish delusion.

Kennedy had ceased to struggle. His mind seemed not to be functioning. He knew he should try to get back to the little island, but he just couldn't swim any more. Exhaustion had caught up with him. It seemed he had reached his breaking point.

He had no idea where the current was taking him. He must be headed somewhere to the north among the Japanese islands, in the dark, wet, chilling night. He untied his soggy shoes from the life jacket and let them sink into the black water. But he hung onto the life jacket and its main burden, the lantern. This was significant, for it seemed to indicate he had not yet given up his will to live. The light might still be valuable as a signal. All the time the current pulled him—first north and east, then gradually east, then verging southeast, then straight south, then at last southwest—through the cold night water of Blackett Strait. He clung to the lantern with grim determination.

That light was a symbol of life and hope, a connecting link with his fellow shipmates back there on the tiny coral island.

When the morning light had washed away the darkness, he saw ahead of him an island which looked exactly like the one he had swum to the previous evening. As he came closer, he was absolutely certain that it must be the same one. He wondered if he was losing his mind. Had he really been moving all night in wind, water and waves, or had he imagined it all?

But one hard fact he knew: dawn was certainly dyeing the gray sky green and, low in the east, orange. He must really have spent the night drifting in the current to the north, into Blackett Strait and back down southeast off the coast of Kolombangara. He reached the small island and found to his great relief that it was the one he thought it was. As he lay on the beach, resting, he tried the lantern and found that it didn't work. He left it there when he got up.

Again he had to resume the struggle to rejoin his crew, but this time he had no shoes.

After crossing the reef, his feet and ankles were blood-raw with coral cuts. And in the dazzling morning sun beyond the reef, the swim across the bay to the home island was agonizing. It seemed to take forever. But this time, there was no local current. He finally reached the home island, with its lace of coconut trees, and crawled up on the beach exhausted. The men saw him and rushed out, surprised to see him still alive. The night's ordeal began to affect his stomach, and he was sick. Though delirious and only semi-conscious, he said clearly to Barney Ross: "Ross—you try it tonight." Then he lapsed into unconsciousness.

That day, while Kennedy lay sick, the men had nothing to do. They talked about their hunger and thirst, and two or three tried to eat the unripe meat of the coconuts and drink the thin, watery milk. It was not a very satisfactory substitute for food. They decided that if they got back to their base alive, they would never again complain about Navy cooking.

Late that afternoon, Ross swam to the neighboring island. He took his .45 to signal with.

Though he spent the night on the reef overlooking Ferguson Passage, no boats passed.

On the morning of August 4, after he had slept awhile, Ross swam back to the home island. The men had named it "Bird Island."

Early that third day, there were planes flying overhead—the enemy's. The men lay low in the bushes. From above they heard the tortured, uneven roaring of dogfights. American planes were tangling with the Japanese in the glinting sky.

By the time Ross staggered up out of the water to report he had seen no sign of any PTs, Kennedy was feeling somewhat better after his night's sleep. He pointed out a larger island to the southwest, nearer Ferguson Passage. It had more coconut trees. Perhaps there would also be some ripe coconuts to slake their thirst and provide some nourishment.

Again Kennedy led the way in the swim, towing McMahon by life-vest straps clenched in his teeth. The other nine men followed, grouped around their plank.

Kennedy and McMahon got ashore safely,

after a three-hour swim. The nine with their raft were caught by a current and carried to the far end of the island. The men reconnoitered cautiously, afraid there might be an enemy detachment stationed there. But they saw none.

Kennedy and McMahon found some coconuts on the ground, broke them open, drank the milk, and were sick. Ensign Thom cautioned the others against drinking too much of the milk too fast.

That night it rained, and McMahon got up to lick the wet leaves of the thick underbrush. In the dark, he bumped into one of his crewmates and stood there paralyzed for a moment, sure that he had run into a Japanese soldier.

The fourth morning was the worst so far, even though the men had gained some nourishment. They were wet, cold and hopeless.

But Kennedy refused to give up. Right on the edge of Ferguson Passage, he spotted a large island he believed was Nauru, from charts he remembered. (Actually, it was Cross Island.) The distance to the island wasn't great. Kennedy and Ross swam it in approximately an hour, arriving in the early afternoon. They climbed ashore very cautiously, afraid of meeting an enemy patrol. Walking was hard for them because both had coral cuts which had swollen like small balloons.

Kennedy and Ross painfully made their way to the Ferguson Passage side of the island. There they moved very carefully, for they saw a damaged Japanese landing barge apparently shipwrecked on a reef. Peering through the brush, they also spied a small rectangular box sitting on the sand farther up the beach. It turned out to be a chest with Japanese writing on its side. In the trees behind the beach, they discovered a thatch shelter, alongside which stood a keg of water and a one-man canoe.

Shortly after this discovery, the Americans sighted two men with a canoe near the damaged Japanese landing barge. They decided the men must be natives because of the way they were dressed. But when Kennedy and Ross tried to attract their attention, the natives hurriedly paddled away from the island.

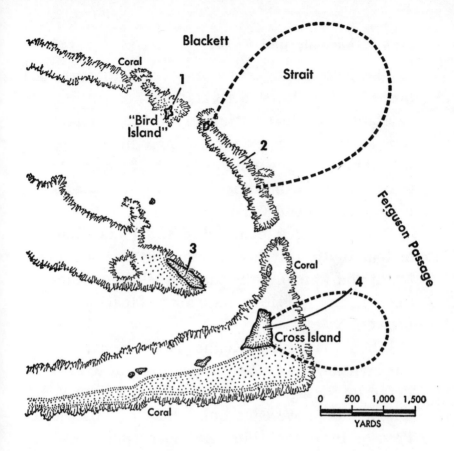

Map of the area where Kennedy and his crew were shipwrecked, showing:

1. The island to which they first swam—"Bird Island."

2. The island to which Kennedy swam (the dotted line encloses the area in which he drifted during his all-night swim).

3. The island to which Kennedy and his crew transferred.

4. Cross Island (the dotted line encloses the area in which Kennedy—and later Kennedy and Ross—paddled with a native canoe).

The two Americans went back into the bushes and sat down to eat and drink something substantial for the first time in four days. (It was now August 5.) They ate sparingly in order to save as much as possible for the men back on the other island. At the same time, they kept a careful lookout for enemy soldiers.

During the rest of the daylight hours, Kennedy and Ross lay low, keeping to the underbrush and watching the thatch shelter, or lean-to, for any possible returning Japanese or natives.

When darkness fell, Kennedy took the narrow, one-man dugout canoe and paddled out toward Ferguson Passage to wait for passing PT boats. Though he hovered around the edge of the Passage for some time, no boats went past. According to the official Intelligence report later released by the Navy, Kennedy then paddled back to Cross Island, where he loaded his canoe with some of the Japanese biscuits and water. Leaving Ross behind, the Lieutenant started for the home island, to take the supplies to his crewmen.

Meanwhile, the two natives whom Kennedy

and Ross had seen near the Japanese landing barge had circled around in their canoe and landed on the island where the rest of the survivors were established. Ensign Thom had done his best to convince them that he and his men were Americans from Rendova. "Americans! Americans! Rendova! Rendova!" he kept repeating with many gestures. Finally the natives seemed to understand and indicated they would do everything possible for the survivors.

The two natives, however, were convinced that there were Japanese back on Cross Island, for they had mistaken Kennedy and Ross for enemy soldiers. When they managed to convey this information to Thom and the others, the crewmen were fearful for their Lieutenant's safety. Thus they were greatly relieved when Kennedy finally appeared with his canoe-load of supplies, which he rationed out to the crew.

The next day, August 6, the natives paddled back to Cross Island with the Lieutenant. On the way they met up with Ensign Ross, who had started to swim over to the home base.

When the group landed on Cross, the natives showed Kennedy where a two-man canoe was hidden. Then the Lieutenant took a portion of a coconut husk and with his pocketknife carved on it in crude, uneven lettering:

                                                    NAURU ISL

               NATIVE KNOWS POSIT
               HE CAN PILOT   1 1 ALIVE NEED
               SMALL BOAT

The natives took the coconut shell, along with a similar message written in pencil by Ensign Thom the previous day. Smiling and nodding agreeably, they pushed off again with their canoe and headed southward.

Kennedy had no way of knowing that the messages would ever get to the right person, so he decided that he and Ross must paddle out into Ferguson Passage again that night to wait for passing PTs. They couldn't depend on the chance that the natives would bring help.

"Skipper, I don't think we can make it," Ross said. His feet were puffed up from coral cuts, and both men were exhausted from the ordeal of the past five days.

But Kennedy had an iron will. "We're going to do it," he insisted. And Ross complied. The two men wearily dragged the heavy dugout across the sand, and were soon paddling toward open water.

As they drew near Ferguson Passage, they were hit by a sudden rain squall. It was a typical August storm in the Solomons with a driving wind, thunder and lightning. Choppy five-foot waves slapped against the canoe.

Kennedy, at the stern, struggled to keep the bow headed into the combers. Ross tried to bail with a coconut shell. Soon even the determined Kennedy saw they couldn't succeed against the storm.

"Better turn around and go back," he shouted. They started to turn the boat, but a white comber caught them broadside and filled the canoe. The two men clung to the boat, which seemed to be drifting toward the open sea.

Kennedy and Ross started to kick their feet to guide the boat in a landward direction. They made painfully slow progress against the storm. The rain swept down in sheets. The night and rain were so thick they couldn't see each other at opposite ends of the boat.

"Sorry I got you out here, Barney!" Kennedy yelled against the storm.

"This would be a great time to say I told you so," Ross responded. "But I won't."

For nearly two hours they struggled to make their way back to the big island. In the storm breakers were smashing over the reef. The force of the breakers turned the men end over end, as if they were turning cartwheels. Ross was seized most violently. The waves banged him hard against the coral. Then they were over the reef, in the lagoon. The two men slowly and painfully made their way over the jagged coral reefs onto the sandy beach. There they collapsed.

Early on the morning of August 7, the weary Americans were awakened by the noise from a small group of natives pulling their war canoe up onto the shore. To their amazement, one of the sturdy Melanesians stepped forward, bowed, and extended a letter, saying in a clipped British accent:

"I have a letter for you, sir."

Scarcely able to believe what was happening, Kennedy took the letter and ripped it open. It said:

ON HIS MAJESTY'S SERVICE

To senior officer, Nauru Island . . .

. . . Have just learnt of your presence on Nauru Island and also that two natives have taken news to Rendova. I strongly advise you return immediately to here in this canoe and by the time you arrive here I will be in radio communication with authorities at Rendova, and we can finalise plans to collect balance of your party.

A. R. Evans Lt.

Will warn aviation of your crossing Ferguson Passage.

Both Kennedy and Ross were beside themselves with joy and relief. Kennedy shook hands with the big Melanesians, and Ross jumped about, slapping them on the back. They all laughed. Ross said it was the first time he had laughed in five days. This was the sixth day since the collision.

Their message, as it turned out, had gotten to an Australian coastwatcher near Wana Wana.

10.

Rescue!

At the war canoe, Kennedy tried to indicate to the natives that he wanted to go to visit the crew. He pointed out the island across the narrow bay, but they were way ahead of him. They nodded, and the leader of the group pointed out cans of C-ration in the boat. Evidently the coastwatcher had sent food for the crew.

Paddling across the bay in the fast war canoe was no chore at all with those muscular backs to drive it along. And at the home island the crewmen shouted and whooped when they heard the good news. The natives pulled a portable stove, cans of C-ration and some yams from the boat and cooked a feast for the crewmen. They also built a lean-to shelter for McMahon, whose burns were now festering badly, and for Ross, whose arm was badly swollen after his beating against the coral.

Kennedy was anxious to be on his way to the coastwatcher headquarters in order to get the rescue of his crew under way. Only one white man would go in the canoe, the natives indicated. There were too many Japanese airplanes flying about to risk more than that in the canoe trip to the coastwatcher's station on the Japanese-held island of Wana Wana. Kennedy was the man.

When the canoe started, the natives indicated that Kennedy should lie in the bottom. They covered him with palm fronds so that, if there were any Japanese planes buzzing around overhead, they wouldn't spot him.

It was a long trip in the afternoon sun, but the natives seemed happy to be bringing their prize to the coastwatcher, as ordered. They pounded on the gunwales to keep time with their strokes, and once they stopped to try to catch a turtle, laughing at the fun of the hunt.

When thirty Japanese planes flew over low, the natives laughed some more at their deception as they waved and shouted cordially at the planes.

It was about 4:00 in the afternoon when Reg Evans, the Australian coastwatcher on Gomu, saw the canoe gliding over smooth water, with apparently only seven natives in it. When it came closer, Lieutenant Kennedy sat up. The Melanesians were still beaming happily at their successful trick of bringing the American officer there through Japanese waters.

Evans took him up to his makeshift base of operations and showed him the file of radio messages he had sent to, and received from, both his own headquarters and that of the PT base at Rendova.

Evans suggested that it would be easy to send Kennedy to Rendova in a canoe. The Rendova PT commanders had already agreed to send PT boats to pick up the crewmen that night. Kennedy could meanwhile be on his way to Rendova. But Kennedy would have none of this. He had firm ideas, still, about what he wanted to do.

First on his list was the rescue of his men. And the rescue would be much easier if he led the PT-boat rescuing party.

Finally, at 6:50 that evening, Lieutenant Evans sent this message to his headquarters, for relay to Rendova:

> Lieutenant Kennedy considers it advisable that he pilot PT boats tonight. He will await boats near Patparan Island. PT boat to approach island from northwest 10:00 P.M. as close as possible. Boat to fire four shots as recognition. He will acknowledge with same and go alongside in canoe. Survivors now on island northwest of Cross. He advises outboard motor. Patparan Island is 1½ miles and bears 214 degrees from Makuti.

The idea of the outboard (and the implied small boat to go with it) was to assist in transferring the injured men and other crewmen to the PT.

At the Rendova headquarters the PT-boat men had at first been somewhat suspicious about the pickup. They wondered if it could be a Japanese trick, to lure them in with some boats and then pounce on them. The Japanese had been known to get on American or Allied radio frequencies and send fake messages. The commanders also distrusted the little native in a dugout canoe who had been sent in by the coastwatcher, bearing Kennedy's message carved in a coconut shell. (This message on its coconut shell, incidentally, was later to hold a place of honor on the President's desk in the White House.)

The PT command finally agreed to send two boats at 10:30 that night to Patparan Island. Kennedy was in the war canoe waiting at about ten o'clock. And two PT boats, commanded by Lieutenant Liebenow and Lieutenant Hank Brantingham, hove up in the darkness off Patparan at about 11:15. Brantingham fired four shots from a .45-caliber by way of a signal.

The men on the PTs heard four answering shots from the darkness: *crack, crack, crack—* then a pause and a deeper-toned, louder bang for the fourth explosion. Kennedy had only three shots left in his revolver, so he had borrowed a captured Japanese rifle from the coastwatcher for the fourth blast. It really was a blast, he told his PT rescuers when they picked him up. He had stood up in the teetering war canoe to fire the gun, and the recoil had almost knocked him into the water.

It was a dark night—no moon—and the native messenger took a place on the bow to guide the lead boat through the islands and reefs.

The boat nosed along in the dark for three or four miles, then the native gave the signal to anchor. The hook was dropped off a reef where waves were breaking, and the crewmen swung a small dinghy into the water. Squadron Commander Cluster climbed in to row, with the native in the bow and Kennedy in the stern. As they approached the shore of the island, Kennedy began to shout for Lenny Thom. "Hey Lenny, where are you?" he shouted. His voice was loud, and Cluster tried to get him not to make so much racket. He was afraid all the Japanese within a hundred-mile radius would hear the shouts. But Kennedy refused to be silenced.

He was raucous, he was flamboyant. After a week of exhausting and superhuman struggle for survival, and the excessive strain and physical

ordeal of acting as leader and—in effect—finding
the leader in himself, he reacted strongly to the
letdown of the rescue.

Kennedy kept yelling while Cluster smiled
and rowed for about a hundred yards. At last
Kennedy heard Thom's voice answering from
the dark. They picked Thom up and rowed him
back to the PT boat.

Then began a shuttle service, during which
Cluster and others of the PT-boat crew worked
up fresh blisters. Cluster was most impressed
with the courage of McMahon. When Cluster
and Kennedy helped him to the dinghy, McMahon didn't utter a syllable of complaint despite
his festering, stinking burns. The other crew
members told Cluster that McMahon had stood
up nobly during the long ordeal, without waver-
ing or feeling sorry for himself.

Soon all the crew members were aboard the
lead PT and it was heading south toward home
—Rendova. The crew reached Rendova PT base
at about dawn, on Sunday, August 8, to find
that a group of war correspondents had already

heard the news and come rushing down to interview the wealthy former-ambassador's son just back from the dead. First, the injured crewmen were taken to sick bay, then there was a session with the Rendova intelligence officers, and after that a press conference.

Kennedy held up very well under the questioning in a tent set up for the interview. He related the story as best he could and still observe the intelligence taboos of an escape story told during wartime. Places and exact means of escape and communication were kept secret, for fear of aiding the enemy.

After the conference he walked out of the tent and ambled to a broken-down army cot under a tree. He was choked up and about to explode with tension. Commander Cluster, his commanding officer in Squadron Two, squatted to talk to him.

Now the accumulated strain of his seven days' ordeal told on Kennedy. He clenched his fists, and tears ran down his cheeks as he told Cluster how the two lost crewmen, Kirksey and Marney,

might have been saved if the other boats of his
formation had come quickly to the rescue.

Cluster tried to calm him down. He explained
that the other boats had seen the explosion when
the destroyer ran down PT-109, and had assumed that the crewmen were all killed. They
hadn't considered, as would veterans of such
experiences, the unbelievable persistence of
human life in surviving the most horrific or-
deals of battle and catastrophe.

Cluster got Kennedy to a bed where he could
recoup in sleep some of his frayed nervous and
physical power. Cluster was already planning to
send Kennedy and the entire crew back to the
States. This was the customary procedure after
a major reverse such as the sinking of one's boat
and the loss of crew members. Kennedy and his
crew had made more than twenty patrols, though
none had been very dramatic until the encounter
with the destroyer *Amagiri*.

Yes, Kennedy and crew had more than done
their duty. And by this time, in the South Pacific,
there were more than enough PT crewmen to go

around. Occasionally there were even enough boats to go around. So Cluster went ahead with preparations to send Kennedy and his crew back to the States for a rest.

II.

"Negative Patrol"

During the second week in August, Kennedy was confined to the Tulagi hospital. He was being treated for infected coral cuts on his feet and legs, and checked for exhaustion, underweight and possible malaria. He didn't tell the doctors about his bad back. His feeling was that, if there were any real trouble, it might interfere with his getting a new command—which he was already thinking about.

While in sick bay, Kennedy ran onto Lieutenant Paul "Red" Fay, the same Fay whom Kennedy had met briefly when Fay was a student and Kennedy an instructor at the PT school in Melville. This time they became good friends. Fay had come down to Tulagi with Commander

Warfield's Squadron Ten, and he had been with them when they were delayed by Japanese torpedoes just outside Noumea, en route to Tulagi.

Fay's boat had been deck-loaded on a tanker carrying four 'Ron Ten PTs. When the tanker was torpedoed, Fay's boat had shot out like a pea from a pod, bow first. The Squadron Ten crews had climbed aboard their boats and taken them off under their own power as the mother ship sank. Eventually they made their way to Tulagi, then Rendova.

It was a story of bravery and resourcefulness, told by the light-hearted Fay with all the good humor such grueling adventures take on as you look back on them.

Talking to Fay helped cement Kennedy's growing resolve to stay at the front and go on fighting. The Lieutenant was also encouraged by an extra bit of good news. He was being recommended for the Navy and Marine Corps Medal for saving his crewmen.

A few days later, after Kennedy's traveling orders had been cut, Commander Cluster was agreeably surprised to find that the fighting Irishman wanted no part of going home. What he wanted was a new command—a new boat to take the place of the 109. And if his crew was being sent home, he wanted another crew to carry the boat into the fight. As Cluster later phrased it: "He got to be more determined—and he was very determined before."

Cluster tore up the orders and began to look around for a boat for Kennedy. He knew of one illustrious craft which would soon be in need of a skipper. She was the PT-59, which had come down to Tulagi before the end of 1942 with Squadron Two. An old 77-footer, PT-59 was nimble and fast. By this time the experienced PT skippers had discovered that the smaller, more maneuverable 77-foot boats had the edge every time over the newer 80-footers, despite the fact that the older boats had less armor plate and less comfortable crew and officers' quarters. The fighting veterans all wanted speed, punch and maneuverability. They didn't mind being less comfortable—or even being less protected by armor plate.

The engines of PT-59 had been lovingly

cared for by Machinist's Mate Homer Facto, and they were something of a legend. The crew that took her to Tulagi, under Lieutenant (j.g.) David M. Levy, kept an open bet of $1,000 that 59 could and would beat any other boat, any time.

PT-59 had already distinguished herself in many actions during the Guadalcanal campaign, when Lieutenant Jack Searles took her on alternate nights with Levy. Then when Searles was sent home for a well-deserved rest, Levy had the boat to himself for several months. Now it was time for Levy to be rotated to the rear, and the boat would be available for new command.

Cluster decided to give her to Kennedy in connection with a new program for converting certain PTs to gunboats. Henceforth these mosquito boats were to be used mainly as gunboats against other small boats, especially the increasingly large numbers of Japanese landing barges coming out of Kolombangara.

The slender PT boats were to be stripped of their torpedoes and tubes, and equipped instead with extra .50-caliber machine guns and 40-millimeter automatic weapons. The old, glorious

David-Goliath mission of attacking destroyers
and cruisers by stealth and speed would be a
thing of the past for all converted PTs.

Accordingly the pennant on the new gunboats was changed. Instead of showing a ram-
paging Disney mosquito clutching a deadly torpedo, the pennant now exhibited a mad winged
bug clutching two giant six-guns, cowboy fashion. The new missions meant a new kind of danger—close-contact fighting in the dark with
automatic weapons along the green coves and
inlets of the Solomons.

Kennedy was enthusiastic when Cluster talked
over his plans to make a gunboat of PT-59. Four
veterans of the original 109 crew would be under
the skipper in the new command: Maguire, the
radio operator; Ed Mauer, the quartermaster;
and machinist's mates Leon Drawdy and Maurice Kowall. (Machinist Mate Ed Drewitch re-
joined the crew later.) Cluster was also giving
Kennedy three men who had served with him:
Christiansen, King and Slagle, all old-time Navy
men and all survivors of the battleship *West Vir-
ginia,* sunk at Pearl Harbor.

In addition, Kennedy would have in his 59 crew Homer Facto, whose engineering skills were legendary, and a good second engineering man, Ed Servatius. There would be new radar equipment on the boat, a skilled radar operator and two regular officers besides Kennedy. She would have fourteen .50-caliber machine guns, two 40-millimeter cannons and a good striping of heavy Class C armor plate, much heavier and much more extensive than anything originally on the boats.

The only catch was that Kennedy and his crewmen would have to do much of the installation of the new gear themselves.

Kennedy plunged into the work like a stevedore, and the men followed his example. The Lieutenant estimated that if they worked at top speed, they could finish in about a month.

"This was probably the hardest physical work that Jack Kennedy ever did in his life," Cluster said of the days when Kennedy and his crew worked on their new boat at the Tulagi base. "The boys worked around the clock in this hot tropical climate."

As the boat neared readiness, Lieutenant Kennedy bragged about his new command and crew. He felt they were more than an equal reincarnation of the sunken PT-109. During this period Kennedy was promoted to full lieutenant from junior grade. By October 9, both the boat and the crew were in tip-top shape, ready to fight or run a boat race. They shoved off from Tulagi for the forward area, Rendova. In accordance with her conversion, PT-59 was now officially known as PTGB-1—Gunboat Number 1.

On October 10, PT-59 arrived in the battle zone. She checked in at the mosquito-boat base at Rendova, though by now there was an advance base beyond Rendova in Vella Lavella, the island most recently assaulted and occupied by American troops. In the swift march of the American attack, Rendova was already becoming a rear-area base, as had happened earlier with Tulagi and the Russell Islands.

In the overall war strategy, the High Command had made its first venture in a new technique which was to accelerate the progress of the Pacific War tremendously: island hopping. Instead of assaulting every successive rung in the chain of Japanese bases, Admiral Halsey and General MacArthur decided to by-pass some of the Japanese strongholds and pounce on less heavily garrisoned islands farther up the chain. They believed that the by-passed garrisons, such as the fortress island of Kolombangara, would be cut off from Japanese reinforcement and supply trains by Allied air and naval supremacy. Given time, these isolated strongholds would eventually be starved out and forced to surrender. Meanwhile, the American forces could be moving on, well up into the islands closer to Tokyo.

Instead of launching a head-on assault at heavily fortified Kolombangara, the next step after Munda, the American amphibious forces jumped beyond to a very lightly held island, Vella Lavella. Vella Lavella was situated in a good spot for a flank attack on the Japanese key position in the Solomons, Bougainville. Supplied and reinforced by American air and sea power, it quickly became the new American (Allied) advance position in the Solomons.

In line with the island-hopping strategy, American PT strength was expected to keep the Japanese from supplying their by-passed island bases. Japanese barge traffic was now heavier than ever before. The Japanese were frantically trying to shore up their northern Solomon positions in Bougainville, Shortland, Choiseul and the Treasuries in anticipation of further American amphibious landings. And almost nightly they were shuttling fleets of barges, loaded with troops, among the islands. The PTs were ideal for intercepting these enemy barges. Practically as soon as the United States Army and Marine forces landed in Vella Lavella, an advance PT base was being set up at Lambu Lambu, on the east coast of Vella Lavella.

Before PT-59 (or Gunboat Number 1) could go on up to the advance headquarters at Lambu Lambu and get into action, there were still some operating difficulties to correct. But by October 17 everything was in first-class shape, and Lieutenant Kennedy reported in at the operations shack of the PT headquarters on Rendova. There he received orders to report the next day for patrol duty out of Lambu Lambu, on Vella Lavella, with five other PT boats. Their mission was to patrol the next night off enemy-held Choiseul Island situated northeast of Vella Lavella, between the new American advance base of Vella Lavella and the key enemy position of Bougainville.

Kennedy's boat was assigned to Section George, along with boats 169 and 183. Their specific job was to "block the western and southern entrances to Choiseul Bay." Section Roger, the other group of three boats, would orbit farther north in the bay.

Kennedy's boat, being first of a new breed of gunboats, was the leader of his section, and carried the section chief, Lieutenant Commander J. E. Gibson. The boat's heavier armament made her the best equipped for the job of barge hunting.

The six boats left Rendova for Vella Lavella at 1:15 P.M., October 18, arrived at the advance PT base at Lambu Lambu about 4:30, and left there well after dark, at nine o'clock, for the Choiseul patrol. It was a bright moonlit night—ideal for spotting barges, and ideal too for being spotted by enemy float planes. Kennedy's boat had a small delay when his center engine began to stutter. He hove to for a few minutes while his machinist's mates tackled the problem. It was solved by some frantic work in the hot, foul-smelling pit of the engine room. About midnight the three boats of George Section edged toward Redman Island, a point of jungle foliage off the southern shore of Choiseul. Their engines were just barely turning over and they were fully muffled.

Kennedy and Commander Gibson consulted in the cockpit. This would be a fair spot to pick up any barges heading to or from Choiseul. They knew that boatloads of troops from Kolomban-gara to the south were still coming into Choi-seul. Intelligence—mostly information from the New Zealand coastwatcher on Choiseul—indi-cated that nearly 5,000 troops had already suc-ceeded in getting to Choiseul from Kolomban-gara. Looking at the dark shape of Redman Island in the moonlight and knowing that a large force of Japanese troops was based right behind it on Choiseul, Kennedy realized that the situation was extremely dangerous. But he tried to keep an appearance of calm. Any moment could bring an outbreak of action as devastating as that which had sunk PT-109 and her crew. He remained tensely alert, ready for sudden moving shadows which might appear beyond the glint of moonlight on the water, or the abrupt roar of an enemy float plane descending from the moon with glittering wings and the shuddering explosion of bombs. Of comfort on this patrol was the new radar set installed in PT-59. Theoretically, at least, it would warn of any enemy surface craft or planes in the vicinity.

As the three boats of George Section crept along, PT-183 and the 59 boat were close together. Boat 183 was to the starboard of 59, and the 169 was off to the left.

At 12:30 A.M. the crew of the 169 boat heard an unmistakable sound—the loud rattling, shivering, shuttling sound of bombs coming down, and the violent *C-R-A-C-C-K! C-R-A-C-C-K!* of two bomb explosions somewhere astern. At almost the same time the crew heard the roar of a plane engine overhead, protesting like a tortured animal as the pilot pulled his aircraft into evasive maneuvers. The crew saw the plane in the moonlight—a single-engined monoplane with a single float. It was well up—more than 2,000 feet—which might have been why the pilot's aim was bad. His bombs had landed far astern of the 169 boat, which he was trying to hit.

The other boats heard the commotion—the blasting of the bombs, the yammering of the machine guns as they tried to get the plane. But a radio check by Commander Gibson showed there were no casualties, and no damage. Kennedy consulted with his radar operator. Why had there been no blip on the radar screen to warn of the approach of the marauder? The radarman had been watching carefully, but there simply hadn't been any blip on the screen. The skipper squinted at the sweeping arm of the radar screen and warned the radarman to keep a sharp lookout.

Commander Gibson conferred with Kennedy, who suggested they might be missing some barge traffic closer inshore to Choiseul. Gibson agreed, and the section moved to within a half-mile of the high, dark mass of the big island. In V-formation, with PT-59 leading and the boats keeping visual contact in the moonlight, the section moved southeast along the enemy coast. But their lookouts spotted no barges; in fact, they saw no sign of life on the dark, jungly shore.

At 1:00 A.M. the radar reported two blips orbiting to the west, at about two miles' distance. The word was passed by radio to the other boats. The gunners charged their weapons; the lookouts scanned the western sky and listened.

But, as the formation crept south along the enemy shore, no bogies were spotted visually or audibly overhead.

When the charts showed the PTs to be off the suspected Japanese terminus called Warrior River, and there was still no sign of an enemy, Commander Gibson decided they had done their stint for the night, and ordered a return to base.

The time was 3:30 A.M. when PT-59, making twenty-seven knots, led the way homeward. The speed was a mistake. Suddenly a roar descended on the boats from the moonlit sky. A plane, un-

spotted by radar, zoomed over PT-183, and a
bomb smashed into the water behind the boat
as the plane screeched over her in a sharp pull-up.

The raid was so sudden that the gunners were
caught off guard. But three minutes later, the
lookouts heard an airplane engine coming again.
A two-engined shape swept screaming over the
183 boat, on the right side of the V. This time
the gunners were ready. The .50-caliber mounts
swept up to their target. As the black, winged
shape grew larger, the tracers leapt toward her.
Then the PT gunners saw red streaks of tracers
coming down from the sky toward them. The
plane was strafing! Then they heard the whish-
ing, shuttling rush of a bomb coming, the shat-
tering impact as it hit between boats 59 and 183,
only a few yards off the 183's port bow. A sheet
of water flooded over the 183 boat. Bomb fragments ripped through the plywood sheeting of
her port side.

On the bow deck of Kennedy's PT-59, Gunner's Mate Christiansen was firing furiously at
the 40-millimeter mount. It was the first of his
guns to go into action. The bell-mouth of the

cannon spat soaring red balls of tracer after the plane as it zoomed up with wings aslant, fleeing into the bright disk of the moon.

Then the plane was gone, without suffering any visible effect from the firing of the two PT boats. Among the PT boats, a quick radio check revealed that there were no casualties and only slight damage—a few holes in Ensign Lewis' 183 boat.

Kennedy's radar screen showed no blips of flying objects in the vicinity of the three PTs. But the crews, having been disagreeably surprised twice that night, were on edge as the boats churned southward toward the PT base at Lambu Lambu.

The six boats of Sections George and Roger reached Lambu Lambu at the first light of dawn, and moored carefully in the bushes so as to be as little visible as possible from the air. Kennedy had to report "negative patrol" at operations headquarters. Despite the frantic and vexing air action, they had not encountered any enemy ships or barges. And that was the only thing that counted. Surface contact was the item which could be listed as a positive patrol, and Kennedy —except for the unfortunate collision with the destroyer on August 2—had not yet in his career as a PT officer had a surface fight.

12.

The End of a Veteran Boat and Crew

During the rest of October, Kennedy plunged back into the dangerous, nerve-fraying, exhausting routine of PT-boat patrols. He was more eager than ever to engage in some action which would give him and his crew a chance to acquit themselves bravely, in the best PT tradition. But for the most part, the patrols were routine, with negative or inconclusive results. This lack of any heroic action made Kennedy impatient and restive. He began thinking of rash enterprises which would get him into the sort of bold action he craved.

Finally one of his commanding officers told him that it was fine to be brave but he shouldn't try to win the war all by himself. This advice from a more experienced man had its effect on the young lieutenant. He learned the wisdom of restraint and good judgment and began to think and plan with a new sense of responsibility. His personal objectives gradually gave way to a greater overall regard for the crew.

When the PT-59 men moved into an accelerated schedule of patrols in Japanese-held Choiseul Bay, the crew members felt his regard for them, and they responded to their skipper's leadership with absolute loyalty. Drewitch spoke for the others when he said, looking back on those days, "We all liked Jack, and would do most anything for him."

By the end of October, Kennedy's PT-59—or Patrol Torpedo Gun Boat Number 1—had still not participated in the kind of derring-do action he yearned for: a traditional PT engagement in the early-Solomons style. But he and the crew had gained something much more important: maturity as warriors. They were becoming professionals, veterans.

The air action in which they frequently engaged was as nerve-frazzling as ever. And even on the negative patrols, where there was no air interception or radar contacts, the threat of sudden attack from above was with them incessantly. It was a psychological hazard that frayed men's nerves, especially when an aggressive skipper like Kennedy kept driving the crew to keep the boat fit and in action. Having endured the nervous tension of a long patrol, they would return to base bone-tired and ragged-nerved to take the boat to a fuel depot for gasoline. Then they would tackle the unending work of cleaning and conditioning, maintaining radio and radar, loading ammunition, briefing for the next mission—and snatch their sleep in spurts of a couple of hours at a time.

The situation in the Pacific had changed again, and the Allied forces were pushing farther up the island ladder in the direction of Tokyo. The effect on Kennedy and the PT boats at Lambu Lambu was mostly indirect, though it involved some honest-to-goodness engagements with the enemy. On October 29-30, eight hundred picked shock troops from Lieutenant Colonel Victor H.

"Brute" Krulak's Marine paratroopers were sent into Choiseul as a diversion—to make as noisy and noticeable an assault as possible. This action was planned solely to convince the Japanese that the main American attack was going to be against Choiseul, not—as actually planned—against Bougainville.

Simultaneously, another amphibious force, composed of Americans and New Zealanders, was directed against Mono Island, in the Treasury Island group to the west of Choiseul. This maneuver was also planned to mislead the Japanese into sending troops in that direction instead of to Bougainville.

The PTs were involved in both of these diversionary efforts. Several of the mosquito boats from Rendova and Lambu Lambu were detailed to take marines into Mono Island. They carried deckloads of scouts, the first troops into the beachhead. For several days running, Kennedy's group was assigned to guard the Choiseul coast, to shoot up and scare off any Japanese reinforcements being moved about by landing barge or even by destroyer. At last the PTs were being let loose on the Tokyo Express, as once before at Guadalcanal. However, the Japanese were running so low on destroyers that they were no longer committing destroyers to cover mere troop movements. They relied instead on landing barges.

Though there were no destroyers, there was comparable desperate action for the fighting Kennedy and his crew. On November 2, PT-59 and two other boats answered an emergency call to go to Choiseul to assist a Marine landing party which was in trouble—a part of Colonel Krulak's parachute battalion. The call was a rare one in that it required action against the enemy in the daytime. And that sort of action was generally taboo. It was considered against the best interests of the night-fighting PTs.

But this was an emergency, and three PT boats, including Kennedy's, left the Lambu base at 4:35 P.M. to head for the northern shore of Choiseul. The assignment was to patrol offshore and keep Japanese surface craft away while three LCPLs (large landing craft for carrying personnel) evacuated a small force of Marine paratroopers driven into a point of land by vastly superior numbers of Japanese troops.

Colonel Krulak's strategy in sending this company of marines into a section far from the main beachhead had been to mislead the enemy into believing that Choiseul was being assaulted by major American forces from several directions. In line with this objective, Krulak had landed the company at the mouth of the Warrior River, in northern Choiseul. His ruse worked, at least for a day and a half. Then the enemy realized it was a feint by a light force, and about 2,000 Japanese pinioned the Marine force on one bank of the Warrior, on the seaward side.

The three PTs arrived on the scene at about 6:20 P.M. The evacuation into LCPLs was already under way with heavy pressure from the foe. The Japanese had massed rifle and machine-gun fire, and a few mortars. They were peppering the overloaded landing craft as they took aboard about fifty troops each, approximately twice their official capacity.

As Colonel Krulak told the story:

The PTs arrived about 6:15 P.M., November 2. The rain was falling and there were long swells in the mouth of the Warrior River. There were only three LCPLs (Higgins boats) to load the company and they were going to overload the boats. The Japs were pushing them, firing with machine guns and rifles.

The boats were crowded with about 50 men on each one. One boat hit a coral head quite a way offshore, maybe 250 yards, and began to sink. Another boat took it in tow, but it was sinking, so some of the boys got on the other boat.

Kennedy's PT boat came alongside and took some of the people aboard, maybe eight or nine. They pulled the bung on the boat that was sinking and let her sink.

There were three wounded among the people Kennedy took aboard. One was Corporal Schnell; he was badly wounded and died on the PT boat.

The PTs stayed with the boats 15 miles south along the coast to Voza [where Krulak's main force were encamped].

So Kennedy had plunged into action, but because of the overall need of the moment he had not fired on the Japanese. Strangely enough, as on the occasion of the sinking of the 109, he had found himself busy saving lives rather than ending them.

Kennedy unloaded his unwounded passengers near the Voza camp in the dark, and they were taken into the beach by an LCPL. From the harried coxswain and the marines, the skipper gained the impression that the Marine beachhead at Voza was close to pulling out. After five days of audacious operations, Krulak's force had achieved its objective—drawing the Japanese off guard with a simulated large-scale amphibious operation. Now it was time to withdraw.

The Krulak force had diverted attention from the real major landing in Empress Augusta Bay, Bougainville. That landing had come off smoothly, on November 1, with no initial ground opposition by the Japanese. Fourteen thousand men (Third Marine Division) and six thousand tons of supplies were put ashore.

But now the Japanese were wise to the Marine deception on Choiseul. They realized that the Krulak force was less than 1,000 in number, and some 5,000 Japanese troops were pressing the small beachhead Krulak had set up around Voza.

The time to evacuate had come, but embarkation waited on the arrival of a fleet of LCIs (landing craft infantry) to take out the marines.

Kennedy, with the dead Marine corporal and the two wounded privates aboard, chugged back across Vella Gulf toward the Lambu Lambu base, in company with two other PTs. It was a good thing that the other two boats were with him, because about 3:00 A.M., PT-59's engines ran out of fuel. Rather than try to transfer gasoline at sea without the proper tools, Kennedy decided to rig a towline to another boat. Proceeding in that fashion, he arrived at the base, where the wounded marines and the one casualty were removed to a doctor's care.

Knowing the situation of the marines at the Krulak beachhead, Kennedy was immediately ready to volunteer for further service. The assignment was quickly forthcoming. PT-59 took aboard a full load of fuel and, after a full day of loading ammunition, conditioning the radar and radio, checking over the engines, and briefing for the night's mission, the boat was under way. At 7:00 P.M. that same night she set out with four other PTs. During the long, arduous night of crossing the bay and patrolling to seaward to ward off enemy surface vessels or planes, the weary skipper hung on in the cockpit and kept his eyes open. Meanwhile the three LCIs ran up on the beach near Voza, lowered ramps and began to take aboard the paratroops.

Shortly before 1:00 A.M., on the morning of the fourth, Colonel Krulak's field headquarters radioed that they were ready to go. The slow-moving convoy started across Vella Gulf, the sleek PTs painfully cutting their speed to their minimum, about twelve knots, with engines in gear and throttles held back, to stay with the LCIs.

It was a wearing, slow, noxious trip, with the responsibility for the safe conduct of the troops resting on the PTs. However, no enemy appeared. The LCIs were safely delivered to the Vella vicinity, and the PTs left them at 5:00 A.M. and reached the torpedo boat base at 5:55.

After mooring in underbrush and debriefing at the headquarters shack, the tireless skipper and his crew were busy with preparations for further action. Though they had completed forty-four straight hours of duty, they filled the PT's tanks with 900 gallons of fuel. Then, at last, they stretched out for a little sleep.

Most of them had a respite that day, but Kennedy was up early to check the engines with Homer Facto—the energetic custodian of the boat's power plant—and to stop at Operations to see what the next stint was going to be. Operations insisted he should take a night off, but the next morning at 8:00 he held a crew muster aboard the gunboat moored in the weeds, and the crew was right in form with no absentees. No wonder he was proud of them, then and since.

The day was November 5, and Operations had a mission for Kennedy. It was a patrol along the southern reaches of Choiseul Bay, in company with PT-187. The mission was a promising one in terms of possible action because there would probably be Japanese barges moving about in the wake of the Krulak raid. It was promising, too, because the two boats were heavily armed. Two other boats would patrol to the south, from Sangigai to Choiseul Bay.

The boats of Kennedy's section went on patrol at about 10:00 P.M. off Moli Island, south of Choiseul Bay. Kennedy led the section, because he was the senior officer. The first hour went by uneventfully. Then, off Moli beach, the lookout sighted three barges hugging the jungly shore. Kennedy maneuvered carefully, trying to get closer. Then he jammed on full throttle. The boat rushed toward the shadowy shapes. Gunner Christiansen blasted away with a short, expert burst of his 40-millimeter cannon on the bow, and Lieutenant North's PT-187, charging along to one side, let go one blast with her 37-millimeter piece. But in a few seconds it seemed that the barges had faded into the black shoreline.

The PTs cruised around the Moli shore trying to contact the barges again. At one point Lieutenant North's radar operator had a blip which could have been a barge, but it vanished.

While they were searching, lookouts heard a plane coming from the north, but it passed over at about 1,000 feet, heading south, without declaring any intentions. Then the boats moved slowly and quietly into Choiseul Bay, cruising around but finding nothing. At last, at 3:00 A.M., Kennedy told Lieutenant North by radio that he wanted to head back to Moli and have another look for the barges. Kennedy was a more mature, wiser warrior now, but he hadn't lost his dogged aggressiveness. He wanted to nail down those elusive barges.

It was 5:30 A.M. and the sky was lighting up in the dawn when the boats reached Japanese-held Moli Island. The islet was forbiddingly clear before them, the trees, rocks, scallops of beach showing in detail. At this hour, patrolling PT boats ordinarily should be reaching home. But Kennedy bored in toward the beach, with PT-187 on his wing, and started a slow circle there, less than 300 yards from shore. He moved his boat fast, the acceptable technique for maneuvers in daylight, and he passed the word for an extra sharp lookout for any movement on the land.

Lookouts picked out six high-prowed Japanese barges along the shore. Three of these appeared to be badly damaged, the others were still serviceable. Here at last were the targets Kennedy had been hoping for. He swung the boat in toward the nearest barge, closing at high speed, and passed the word to commence firing. He had already made a plan for maximum destruction to the enemy with minimum risk to his crew. He would swing close to the two nearest barges, then curve seaward evasively so that the farthest barge, on the northern point of Moli, could be reached by long-range fire.

The two rushing PTs swept shoreward toward the nearest barge. Christiansen and King, at the bow and stern 40-milimeter mounts, let go with carefully aimed blasts. The tracers streaked, curved into the first barge. White puffs showed where some of them detonated on the hull. Pieces flew as the shells hit; rips were visible in the side as the 59 boat roared by. Some crewmen reported smoke rising from the enemy hull.

The two PTs charged along the beach toward the second Japanese landing boat, which was lined up like the first with its prow toward the two onrushing American craft. So far there had been no answering fire from the enemy, but at any minute a cross fire from a dozen machine gun emplacements could open up from behind the trees.

Kennedy held in close at speed and Christiansen did his part, blasting at the second barge with his 40-millimeter. Pieces flew from the enemy's prow. Now the scooting 187 boat had got her 37-millimeter gun into action. It, too, was firing fast.

There was still no answering fire from the enemy shore. But the enemy, if he had any capability, had had enough warning, and the visibility was good. It was 6:00 A.M. and the dawn was bright. Kennedy knew these factors well and had calculated them in advance. Now he carried out the curve of his attack, veering away from the beach, but only enough to bring his boats away from the range of possible shore emplacements near the two barges. The planned course of the two PTs gave both gunners a clean shot at the third enemy barge, from about 400 yards. The gunner on PT-187, closer on this shot than Christiansen, saw a handful of PT shellbursts tossing smoke puffs over the enemy hull, making pieces fly. His later report, when the boats got back to Lambu, said there were seven or eight hits on this third barge, and that these "rendered it unserviceable."

In the next twelve days, the crew of PT-59 (Gunboat 1) and their skipper were really hitting their stride. Like a good team at the end of the season, they were at the top of their form. But as with any great team in top form, they were wearing toward the exhaustion that comes with maximum effort. So it was with the fighting skipper and the fighting crew of Boat 59.

The logbooks tell this story in swift compass: the story of long, grueling patrols conducted with maximum efficiency, of keeping the boat always in shape so that it could be ready for the next night, of consideration among the crew members for each other, of working expertly with other boats, whatever the job.

There were many nights recorded—of long patrols during which both crew and boat kept operating at top readiness. And there were nights too when the skipper, crew and boat gave a worthy account of themselves in action.

In those November days, when the marines were fighting hard to take over Bougainville, the PT-59 (Gunboat 1) and her crew were turning their cog in the war machine, searching out enemy barges, ferrying troops into and out of dangerous areas, and shooting off Japanese night-flying float planes.

But the night-and-day duty and the living in primitive, unhealthy conditions and the never-ending nervous strain of having to function under the shadow of death and injury, were taking their toll.

On November 11 Gunner King, who had so ably manned the stern 40-millimeter mount, had to leave the boat with painful stomach trouble. On November 15 two other gunners, W. C. Cline and the redoubtable Christiansen, were sent into sick bay. And at last, on November 18, the leader of the fighting body, Lieutenant John F. Kennedy, "left the boat, as directed by Dr. at Lambu Lambu." Kennedy's ailments, as accumulated in nine months of service with the front-line PTs, were malaria, a bad back, which had been worsening since the ramming of the PT-

109, and severe undernourishment. He had
dropped twenty-five pounds from his spare frame
since his arrival at Tulagi. Also, he was on the
point of exhaustion—mental and physical. Many
had gone this way in the course of the Solomons fighting, wearing themselves to the finest
of edges, and beyond.

So Kennedy was again ordered to sick bay at
Tulagi, in the former tribal chieftain's house,
which had been converted to a hospital. "It was
a hard blow to him to leave the boat with most
of the crew on board," Homer Facto said later.

But the rest of the crew were soon to be relieved en masse. The new PT flotilla leader,
Commander W. C. Specht, heard about their
record, and saw the sad physical state of Homer
Facto when Homer made a visit to Calvertville.
The team which had worked so well with their
young skipper was retired to rest in a rear area.
Perhaps, if the war went on that long, they would
someday see another season in a combat zone.

The 59 boat, proud old-timer that she was,
and veteran of far more action than any of her
crew members, still had plenty of life and fight

in her. She was shifted to the new PT base at Green Island, one of the islands seized by the advancing American forces in the Bougainville campaign. From Green Island, she was moved ahead to more forward bases of the South Pacific as American forces advanced toward the Philippines. Finally old age (which comes too fast to boats) caught up with her. Like an old campaign race horse sent out to pasture, she was turned over to the Army Transport Service, her guns removed, to serve out her last years as a launch.

Homer Facto, after his leave for rest and recuperation, was assigned to a new PT squadron, 'Ron 38, in New York. He heard that the old 59 boat had been brought to Manhattan as an Army ferryboat. He went to the slip on the East River where she lay, badly in need of paint, repair, and the kind of human care he used to bestow on her—and he couldn't stand the sight. He had to leave. "I had to leave disheartened, I guess you would call it."

The crew members had their rest and rehabilitation, like Homer Facto, and with the war's end were reconverted to civilians. The marvelous human frames, hearts and minds of the trained PT veterans were done over into new guises, with a degree of reconversion that could never happen to a boat. They scattered into many different parts of the country in many different jobs. Homer Facto became proprietor of Facto's, a billiard parlor and tobacco shop at Ausable Forks, New York. Maguire was metamorphosed into an official of a loan company in Jacksonville, Florida. Drewitch built up his own building supply firm in Urbana, Illinois. And so it went. As for the skipper, Lieutenant John F. Kennedy—well, everybody knows what happened to him.

Index